Bill

SOUL SEARCHING

journeys into spirit

FR. JOE HENNESSY

Amor
DEUS
PUBLISHING

Soul Searching
Journeys into Spirit
Father Joseph Hennessy

Cover and Inside pages photos: Fr. Joe Hennessy
Cover and book design: Amor Deus Publishing Design Department

For information regarding permission, write to:
Amor Deus Publishing
Attention: Permissions Dept.
4806 South 40th Street
Phoenix, AZ 85040

Paperback:
ISBN 978-1-61956-129-8
Hardcover:
ISBN 978-1-61956-133-5

Second Edition May 2014
10 9 8 7 6 5 4 3 2 1
First Edition printed June 2013 by Tau Publishing, LLC.
Published and printed in the United States of America by Amor Deus Publishing,
Amor Deus Publishing and Tau Publishing are imprints of Vesuvius Press
Incorporated.

❄ **Dedication** ❄

I thank my parents for their gifts.
Faith from my Mom, Mary Ellen,
and the great gift of wonder from my Dad, Pat.

From my Mom, I learned my prayers.
My Dad taught me to look beyond the outside
and look to the inner person.

I received my understanding and practice of religion from my Mom.
From Dad came the gift of seeking out the new, being open to the not yet,
and knowing that life is to be lived and lived to the fullest.
And to my sister, Virginia, who was my little mother.

At that time, I did not know or understand,
but now I am beginning to understand.

❊ Acknowledgements ❊

"Life is a process," so we are told. Well, the same can be said about this book. I am a speaker not a writer. Some people will say I speak at great length. I mention this, so that when you come across errors in grammar and sentence construction, I'm asking for your understanding or even empathy. To write a book was never part of even my wildest dreams. However, over the years, when I was encouraged to write by several friends, I resisted the idea. When I retired, Fran Matera and Lisa Amato ganged up on me one day at lunch. This resulted in no book, but instead a weekly blog. At that time, I still wasn't able to type. No problem; Lisa volunteered to type. Then after three years, Fran began the process of putting the blogs (2009-2013) together, the result is this book.

I read that everything written about the spiritual life is plagiarism; I concur. I will not be writing anything that will be radically new. You will be familiar with the material and all I hope to do is to offer you a new set of lenses leading to seeing beyond what is the ordinary and familiar. Over the years, I've sat at the feet of many "Masters" who have greatly influenced my thinking. Some of these "Masters" include Thomas Merton, Henri Nouwen, Carl Stuhmiller, John Shea, Eugene La Verdiee, Eugene Kennedy, Anthony de Mello, Esther de Waal and Ronald Rolheiser to mention a few.

I would like to thank Fr. John Coleman, Fr. Gary Ragula, Shelly Connors and the editors of their respective publications for making space available on a weekly basis. To my Facebook Friends, and you who have followed my almost weekly blog, thank you. Your support has been so encouraging.

Thank you to Vinnie Smith for allowing Belinda Chron Boydston to work on this project, while she was in his everyday employment. Belinda continued to work on the material and had a great impact on the final document. To Kimberly Pope, thank you for your contribution. I would also like to thank Elaine McElroy for her constant patience with the many, many changes. My deep gratitude to Mick McLaughlin for doing the final editing. This is the fruit of a long journey; let it continue. Thank you for joining in and becoming part of the eternal process.

To Jeff Campbell at Tau Publishing and his staff for taking the risk and publishing this book.

Blessings to and on all,
Fr. Joe

❈ Foreword ❈

It is a distinct honor to write a foreword to this very engaging book authored by my friend of 54 years. We both came off the same ordination assembly line on June 8, 1963. Fr. Joe's *Soul Searching: Journeys into Spirit* with its many hiking metaphors, stories and images reveals a daring outer and inner exploration of *Aisling*: God's dream for us. It is deeply personal and autobiographical. Its style is transparent and brutally honest. It appears that Fr. Joe, the hiker, is an incurable nature mystic. Surely, this explains his love for God's book of creation. His faith experiences, related so well in these pages, are testimony a-plenty to his encounter with the Holy in *Lectio Divina* from the book of creation.

I hope each reader will find it as engrossing, enlightening, and instructive as I did. As I read through it in one sitting, I felt like I was looking into a mirror and seeing myself with all my vulnerabilities in my own soul searching journey. I enjoyed the distillation of wisdom from Fr. Joe's life experience, and the integration of insightful and meaningful quotes from a wide range of authors. I am deeply touched and grateful for the holistic message and spirituality of this book.

May all who experience the Holy through encounter with God's dream of us be enlightened by this book and be similarly blessed and come to know what it means to be the beloved of God.

Tomas O Cathalain
Our Lady Mother of Sorrows
Tucson, AZ
Author of The Heart of the Poet

❧ Contents ❧

Introduction:	1
Chapter 1: The Journey	5
The Sacrament of…Reading	9
Nature's Gifts	11
Either/Or vs. Both	13
Celebration	14
Chapter 2: Rocks & Refuge	17
The Cocktail	19
Three Gifts	21
Shower…of…Shalom	22
Live & Learn	24
Chapter 3: GPS: God's Persistent Safety Net	29
Continuous Persistence	30
How Many Chances	31
Staying Alive	33
The Saboteur	34
The Trash-Talker	35
The Truth-Speaker	36
Choosing A Path	37
Chapter 4: A Question of Time	39
Hanging on…in Faith	40
Receiving to Give	41
Compassion	42
Blind Alley	43
Toxic Shame	45
From Fear to the Freedom of Faith	48
Reconciliation and Guilt	52
Toxic Trinity	53
Free Will or Won't	57
Chapter 5: Up the Mountain	61
Acceptance	62
Feeding the Spirit	64
God Walks His Talk	65
Chapter 6: Switchbacks	69
Divine Encounter	70
Life Happens	71
Failing and Falling	73
Chapter 7: Thrown for a Loop: End & Begin Again	75
Blessings	76
Hope	78
Become a Butterfly	80
Mother…Motherhood…is a Sacrament	81
Epilogue: Moving On	85
About The Author	87

❆ Introduction: ❆
Aisling: God's Dream for Us

The word *Aisling* will be a word not familiar to you. It is the Irish or Gaelic for *dream*. We are the result of God's dream. We are here on earth living out the dream that God had of us since before time existed. So, we have emerged from the mist of eternity, The Eternal.

God's dream for us is that we would have life and have it to the fullest, yet this is not our experience. It is not our reality. In some instances, we sabotage God's dream for us ourselves. At other times, we enable other people to be the instruments in us losing sight of the dream and settling for less.

Aisling on Earth will be an effort to bring home that "each one of us is not a human being seeking a spiritual experience, rather we are spiritual beings immersed in the human experience." (From Pierre Teilhard de Chardin) As Shakespeare said in Hamlet, "Aye there's the rub." From Johannes Metz in *Poverty of Spirit*, we learn, "we are born human and spend our whole lifetime discovering what human means." The Latin word for earth is *humus* and it is from that we get the words *humanity* and *human*. We are the dream of God, which is being lived out in and through the human experience.

On this journey, on this hike, we are led into the mystery of who we are, who our God is and who we are, in relationship with one another and all of creation. The purpose is to take a wonder-look at your life, my life and all of life. To take a wonder-look at all that is created, all that is real. With this wonder-look, I hope what will be revealed is the real person behind each person, the real story behind each story, and ultimately The Reality behind all reality. This will take a great amount of courage, trust and Faith. We never journey alone, our God is always journeying in us, with us and through us for others. "In Him we live, we move and we have our being. Each day He shows us His love which is the power of the Holy Spirit in our lives." (*Catechism of the Catholic Church*).

It is easier to understand what St. Francis said, "Everything that is, is to be adored" and de Chardin says, "By reason of creation and still more by reason of the incarnation there is nothing profane for him/her who knows how to see."

I hope this new understanding will lead you to a new awareness which in turn may excite you to an ever-deepening "YES" to life as it is being encountered in the here and now.

We do not meet life, we encounter life. Encounter brings with it the reality of change, something new is present. Our God says to us in Isaiah 43, "See, I am doing something new! Now it springs forth, do you not perceive it?" In time we each have to look at the lenses through which we see life and come to realize our lenses are not always clear. Lent is a great time to clear the lenses and be able to see more clearly the mystery of God being revealed to us in each and every person, place and event of our daily life. Hopefully, we will then be led to look beyond the obvious to the unseen, to the mystery beyond. This place of mystery, the beyond, is our true home.

We begin our journey with no idea where we are going. We are seekers on a trail strewn with many more questions than answers. We maneuver around the GARBAGE – guilt, anger, resentment, boredom, anxiety, greed, envy – that is central to our quest. If we take it upon ourselves to act as our own savior, we fail miserably, stumbling into dysfunction represented by a "toxic trinity." We trip over the deception that Hell is inevitable when God's Dream is just the opposite – it's easy to go to Heaven and difficult to get into Hell.

Jesus is a rescuer, a kinsman redeemer, a sacrifice to bridge the gap between Heaven and Earth. He illuminates the dark night of our souls (knowledge) and our senses (feelings). When we acknowledge Him and His truth, then the more lost we are, the greater our chances are of being found, not abandoned.

Soul Searching: Journeys into Spirit is a guide to a more authentic, personal encounter with His creation. Each chapter offers a glimpse of our life's work – a mysterious journey filled with obstacles, challenges, questions, answers, fact, fiction, time outs, peaks, valleys, falls, failures, lessons learned and ultimately – moving on to a new reality.

The following is my understanding of what takes place in each and every moment we are given to live. These are the choices you and I are challenged to make so that we can live in the freedom of being the beloved daughter/son of our gracious Prodigal Father.

The Battlefield of the Soul

MY FREE WILL:
Given out of Love

<u>Toxic Trinity</u>		<u>God's Dream - The Aisling of God</u>

The Father of Lies	........The saboteur ....The prosecutor ....Sarx (Paul's Flesh)	The Holy Trinity	........Father ....Son ....Holy Spirit

I CHOOSE
EVERY MOMENT

Control	Power	Hatred	Earn	Guilt		Faith	Light	Unconditioned	Wisdom	Time
Comparison	Property	Violence	Deserve	Fear		Hope	Life	Unlimited	Empowerment	Attention
Competition	Prestige	Death	Qualify	Shame		Love	Love	Unrestricted	Transformation	Tenderness

Death Dealer-Victim-Wounded Wounder   Wounded Healer-Survivor-Life Giver

**Oh God, help me to believe the truth about myself
No matter how BEAUTIFUL it is.**

As you have been given, so you want to give back. I was on Logan Pass in Glacier National Park. I was on the way up on the path to the lake. I noticed a hiker ahead who had stopped and was leaning against a rock. It was obvious she was finding the hike difficult. As I approached, she said, "I cannot keep up the pace of the others." I found myself saying, "You are going to get there in your own time and at your own pace, not the way your friends are going to get there." I moved on.

In time, we each must examine the lenses through which we see life and realize our lenses are more cloudy than clear. God is revealed to us in each and every person, place and event of our daily journey in the eternal now. With grace, we can learn to look beyond the obvious of the seen, to the unseen. This place of mystery — the beyond, the unseen — is our true home.

❧ Chapter 1: ❧
The Journey

"Me thinks that the moment my legs begin to move,
my thoughts begin to slow."
— HENRY DAVID THOREAU

When I first came to America, like all the Irish priests, I played golf every week. And I did so on a regular basis for many, many, many years. As I got older, things began to change in my body and eventually I had to give up playing golf. In order to make up for the lack of exercise, I began walking around the St. Andrew the Apostle campus, which led to walking around the neighborhood, and then eventually expanded into hiking. I developed a great love for hiking. Now today ,hiking has become an essential part of my daily and weekly routine. Each hike is different yet familiar. However, I believe, that whatever we look at long enough, a message breaks through beyond the obvious. Often it's because while things are familiar, we really never get to know them. There exists a deeper reality beyond the reality we see. He who is unseen enables us to connect with a deeper reality on an ever-deepening level, and ultimately with all that is, and with all creation.

G.W.F. Hegel writes, "Generally, the familiar, precisely because it is familiar, is unknown." I felt a certain sadness when I first read that quotation. How often do we take what is familiar for granted? When we take something for granted, we do not show it much respect or reverence. It appears to have no value for us. This "take-it-for-granted attitude" deprives us of the wonder-fullness of all that is in our everyday life. I believe what St. Francis says: "There is nothing profane for him/her who knows how to see." Gerald Manley Hopkins expresses this so well when he tells us that "all of creation is charged with the grandeur of God."

More than 60 million people hike in America. This multitude immerses themselves in the grandeur of the cathedral we call the great outdoors. But with what result?

Speaking for myself, there have been very few times I have come off a hike without being in some way changed. When I encounter another part of creation, namely nature, something is different. Creation meets creation in this encounter. The presence of the Creator dwelling within each one of us reaches out and connects in a mysterious way. This encounter always leaves us aware there is something more in us, and we want to connect with it. This "something more," this Other, cannot be explained, defined or communicated through the medium of words. Words are limiting and God is limitless.

What we want to communicate is our encounter with mystery. We can never understand or explain mystery. Neither can we exhaust its meaning. All we can do is have reverence for it, and allow mystery to speak to us. It speaks, speaks, speaks and never exhausts itself.

With no offense to M. Scott Peck, life is not a road to be traveled. Rather it is a hike to be taken. With each part of a hike completed, I become more aware of the deep connection between what I have just experienced and my ongoing understanding of the spiritual life.

When we hike a trail, it offers many twists and turns. It will have ups and downs. On the trail, we will meet all sorts of stones. Some are little; some are big. We call the big ones rocks. Some are flat and a comfort to our feet. Others are sharp and pointy; they threaten the comfort of our feet. These latter ones awaken us to the need to be more careful, more particular about where we step. Some of the larger rocks must be navigated either over or around with care. We are always making decisions about which is the right way to go. We ask ourselves, which is the way that is not too risky or too dangerous?

With each step we take, we make a decision. Which is the way that is healthy and good for us right now? The spiritual life is ever and always about the present. It does not matter what has happened in the past. The past is over. What does matter is how we attend to the now. That is why there is that great similarity between hiking and the spiritual life. In both, all we have is this moment; this step. There is no other way to make progress along the trail except through taking this one step. In the spiritual journey, all we have is the here and now. There is no other way of encountering God – of encountering the mystery – except by our attention to " the right now." Hence, we have the *sacrament of the present moment.*

"The Eternal silence of these boundless faces strikes awe in my soul."
—PASCAL

When we are on a trail, we know it's just us and the trail. The trail welcomes us with no judgment, no conditions, no restrictions. It opens before us all the possibilities. We will only walk the trail once. Every hike is unique; one of a kind.

Although I have hiked some trails many times, each time I begin the hike I bring what has previously happened to me, making this hike a new encounter between the person on the last hike and all that has happened since. There is the challenging reality of experiencing a new

6

me as I place one foot in front of the other.

The trail will be shared at times, and then intersect with the trail of others. This is good, necessary, and helpful. One day I was on a hike in the mountains outside of Estes Park. It was a trail I had never hiked before. I had no idea how difficult it would be. The trail kept getting steeper and steeper. I was beginning to move slower and slower. I noticed when I get into a situation such as this, I don't take long strides but revert to baby steps. With those baby steps I can make my way higher and higher. I met a fellow hiker. He was on the way down the trail. He looked at me, then with a big, warm, encouraging, welcoming smile (he must have been Irish), he offered these words of encouragement: "It's not far now, and it's worth it." Those words somehow picked me up. I got a little of my strength back in my step, and I completed the hike. Yes, it was worth it.

As we have been given, so we want to give back. On Logan Pass in Glacier National Park, I was on the way up on the path to the lake. I noticed a hiker ahead who had stopped and was leaning against a rock. It was obvious she was finding the hike difficult. As I approached, she said, "I can't keep up the pace of the others." I found myself saying, "You're going to get there in your own time and at your own pace, not the same way your friends are going to get there." I moved on.

Later, while driving down "The Road to the Sun," I was stopped in a long line of traffic. We were going nowhere. I got out of my car to enjoy the fantastic scenery. Then I heard somebody say "There is my encourager." It was the lady from the hike. She and her friends were united. That began a joyful conversation. As we say in Ireland, "The Craic was mighty." After a time, the traffic moved on and we separated never to meet again. Yet from that encounter, gifts were given and received. These moments we call moments of grace.

How often do we find ourselves in similar situations in everyday life. These situations reflect our spiritual life. But how often when we need encouragement or some kindness do we receive it? Often, people we meet will not only pass us by but blow by us. They blow by us as if we were invisible. They are so engrossed and wrapped up in their own agenda that the wonder of others and of all creation is sadly missed. They focus on the little picture of their narrow glimpse, losing out on the wonder-full exciting picture that is all creation.

On the other hand, there are hikes where we receive greetings and smiles. We hear, "Hi, how are you?" "Great day!" "Wow, this is wonderful!" "Have a good one." "Joy." One summer day while I was hiking on Phoenix's South Mountain, I frequently heard the comment: "I cannot believe this is June." When you respond with a comment, it often leads to an extended conversation. You are acknowledged even if for a brief moment. Other people we meet on the hike really listen and pay attention to your comments. Strange as it may be, when we meet them again, there's a welcome and recognition. It is this atmosphere of hospitality that makes a hike a wonder-full, warm, freeing experience. In this, we receive encouragement to move on and on and on.

Hikers will greet us *from where they are* and meet us *where we are*. I was on one of my favorite hikes in the Tetons when I noticed a mature couple coming towards me. They walked slowly together in obvious harmony. They exuded a comfort with themselves and where they were. (Most mature couples have that gift). They were dressed like they belonged on the front cover of a hiking magazine. I saluted them with my usual greeting, "How are you doing?" In a very peaceful, rich, and calm voice came the response, "Uniquely." What a great answer. I was so taken aback by their response that I was stuck for words to say.

Uniquely is the way we all go through life. We tell our own unique story in the unique living of every moment, of every day of the life we are given to live. The unique part of God's story is incarnated in *our* unique story revealed in the space each one of us is placed. When we fail to get in touch with our uniqueness, we betray our own special giftedness. We are then unable to fulfill our God-given destiny. The result is a deeper awareness of our emptiness, our loneliness, and a great sense of being disconnected. To be other than who we truly are is a denial of the wisdom of God and a disbelief in His creativity. God does not make copies. God does not duplicate. We copy; we desire to be someone other than who we really are because we either do not know who we are, or we don't want to know. Or in some cases, we are afraid to know. We must always keep in mind that we are created from God's love through His freedom.

"The trees, the animals, the streams, the flowers,
preserved as much as possible in their natural state of beauty,
will in turn help preserve our most precious resource — the human spirit."
—LAURANCE S. ROCKEFELLER, *June 12, 1955*

We are always on a journey of discovery; a journey into our unique selves. There is a certain aloneness – loneliness – in being unique. We have no one with whom to truly connect except He who is the source of our uniqueness: God. He Who Is Alone.

Out in the wilderness we have none of the everyday medicators to distract us from our disturbing feelings. These feelings arise again and again. They apparently have a will of their own. Like all feelings, we have to process them in order to deal with them. We have to experience them, express them, let go of them, and then most importantly, welcome God into the emptiness of the letting go. With the letting go there is a vacuum – a void that if God does not fill it with His love, evil will have that space all to itself.

We are told that neither the physical nor the spiritual realm can tolerate a vacuum. It is always our choice whether to choose God's presence and God's grace. His love is always there to fill the void. And we each respond uniquely to God's grace in our own special way. God gives us a special grace, and we in turn can become (sometimes painfully) the "me" God knows and loves. We are always invited to respond to His creative love – the Holy Spirit. However, when we refuse that invitation, we respond out of our ego which leads to destructive living.

If our response to the question, "How are you doing?" is always "Uniquely," what a difference it would make in our own world and in the world of the people we encounter. It would make people stop and really take notice of who we are and from where we are coming. When we answer "Uniquely," we are not the person they think we ought to be, nor whom they expect us to be. We are not whom they want us to be. In that answer, we are expressing our uniqueness and recognizing they, too, are unique. Hence, because they are not us, they have a different unique being, so they will never understand completely what we think, say, or do. What they can do is respect and revere our uniqueness because this is God's unique gift to us.

We do not choose to be unique. The more that I am who I really am in God's mind, the more I am contributing to God's unique special plan for all of creation. God has chosen you and me from all eternity to hike our own special trail – the awe-full, lonely, difficult trail of uniqueness.

The Sacrament of…Reading

Summertime is a time for reading and relaxation. People stock up on their "beach books," and "travel books." Some of these books are meant for escape. While others are meant for inspiration. It is good to have a balance. I always encourage the hard working and the driven to read a book, or books, that have no redeeming value whatsoever. Sounds good? I have always loved the journeys I was, and am taken on, by so many different authors.

I have mentioned before that I travelled many Arizona trails, even before I became an Arizonan. Zane Grey has always been, and continues to be, my very favorite author. I now have to think, and for the FIRST time, how much of my reading of westerns went into my decision to volunteer for the old Diocese of Tucson. Up to now I had always thought, I volunteered after I read of the ratio of priests to Catholic, one to 12,000. (I read that statistic in 1957 in the library at St. Patrick's College, Carlow.) The mind...when are we ever going to understand its mystery? Not in our lifetime, that I know. In my wondering, I have wandered, and for those who have heard me in person you say, "What is new?"

So back to where I left off, reflecting on books. Inspirational books are an essential, and necessary part of a library. We need to be challenged to leave behind our narrow way of thinking. Our unchallenged minds will lead us to that comfortable place where all we do is vegetate. In that place of comfort we will have the audacity to be the judge and jury of ourselves, and consequently, of those we deem lesser than we. We become so self-righteous and condemning. Let us be gentle and understanding here. We are not acting from a place of real truth, we are acting out of our ignorance. As we are led from ignorance, by grace, into a deepening understanding of the whole truth of who we really are, something drastic, mind-blowing happens. A change in perception happens. We are led into the truth of who we really are in the freedom of God's love. We are asked, even challenged, to start the journey into the belief of a love that is beyond our limited, human imagination.

We have to let go, and this is so scary, of all that is familiar to us, and journey, somewhat naked, into the unknown. Is not *The Unknown*, another name for God? How awe-full is that? Worth the pain and the struggle? Nothing in the spiritual life comes to us, without FIRST having to endure a journey into our brokenness, our innate powerlessness and gut wrenching fear. I read this many years ago, and I use it so often myself, and encourage so, so many to make this part of their daily prayer, and reflection.

> "And now God says to us what He has already said to the world as a whole through His grace-filled birth: I am here. I am with you. I am your life. I am your time. I am the gloom of your daily routine. Why will you not bear it? I weep your tears, pour out your tears to Me. I am your joy. Do not be afraid to be happy forever, since I wept, joy is the standard of living that is really more suitable than the anxiety and grief of those who think they have no hope. I am the blind alleys of all your paths, for when you no longer know how to go further away, then you have reached Me, though you are not aware of it. I am in your anxiety, for I have shared it by suffering it. And in doing so, I wasn't even heroic according to the wisdom of the world. I am in the prison of your finiteness, for my love has made me your prisoner. When the totals of your plans and life experience do not balance out evenly, I

am the unsolved remainder. And I know that that remainder which makes you so frantic, is in reality my love that you do not understand. I am present in your needs. I am there and they are now transformed, but not obliterated from my heart. I am in your death, for today I began to die with you, because I was born, and I have not let myself be spared any part of this death....Ever since I became your brother, you are as near to Me as I am to myself." Karl Rahner, *Blind Alleys - Search*

What awe-full, wonder-full words these are. Great fodder for thought as one sits and relaxes by the gentle surf, or by a babbling mountain brook. Words that must be allowed to travel deep and into the depths of who we are, so they can be mingled with what has already penetrated to those depths. Of late we have sung, in prayer, "I will come to you in the silence, I will lift you from all fear, you will hear my voice. I claim you as my choice, be still and know I am near." Do we believe that reality? How awe-full is that? We have to wonder, and wonder at those words and allow whatever to surface and be owned.

There is a new country song, at least new to me, with the words "I love that you love me." We can add "God" here to make a personal prayer owning the deepest reality of who we are. It provides us with limited words as we struggle to express the inexpressible. In prayer we are always coming up short. Is that not the reason we have The Spirit within to do that which we desire, but of ourselves cannot accomplish. The desire to pray, IS to pray. This is a fact we must always keep before us. Spiritual reading is a great "starter" of prayer. Hence it is called sacramental. (That is "sacrament" with a small "s." My definition of sacrament is: each and every person, place, event, action, in fact all reality, that brings us into contact with the deeper realities of life, and ultimately with Reality Itself. That Reality we call God.) Consequently, wherever we are really present, this is the place we encounter The Sacred, The Other, The Unknown, The Ineffable. That is why, wherever you stand, you are always standing on Holy ground.

"Life has got a habit of not standing hitched. You got to ride it as you find it. You got to change with it. If a day goes by that does not change some of your old notions for new ones, that is just about like trying to milk a dead cow."
—WOODY GUTHRIE

Nature's Gifts

There is a great peace in nature; a great quiet in the wilderness. In nature, the silence gives us pause. You don't meet too many couples fighting or arguing as they hike. Sometimes the only fight I am aware of is between me and myself. There is a great healing gift offered to us by nature. I remember a number of years ago, on one of my vacations, I wasn't doing very well. I was not in a good place. My entire vacation was spent in the woods, lakes, mountains and on the seashore. That vacation was not an easy one to endure because I wasn't looking forward to returning to the challenge of everyday living.

However, when I returned from my vacation, I was surprised, even shocked, to find out that I had a new attitude, a new energy, a new enthusiasm for life and for work. When this gift was given to me, I do not know. All I do know is when I returned, there was a difference. Later, I read in a John O'Donohue book that "nature heals you by itself." Nature draws out, but only over time, that essential goodness deep within each one of us.

This essential goodness is just waiting to be experienced and to be released in order to enhance the goodness of all of creation.

I further noticed over the years that, when on vacation, the more I faced difficulties and challenges with myself, the better I was able to handle the challenges when I returned to that life we call "normal." I have never known how this happens, but I have met other people who have had the same experience.

Ever watch couples, families, groups caught up in the viewing of an ocean sunset? As the sun slowly slides beneath the horizon of our world and our vision, it is telling us another day is ending. When people are in the presence of an ending, whatever it may be, somehow they move a little closer. Arms are extended. Couples are joined and children huddle a little closer to their parents. Arms entwined, people encircled in a very reverential silence. Each one is somehow left alone to be with who they really are at that moment. There is a special moment; a moment of silent awe, a moment of silent wonder. Hence, it is indeed a moment of grace. We are praying.

The human spirit is somehow enhanced, transformed, liberated, and excited as it experiences the mystery and the majesty to be encountered in the "cathedral of the great outdoors." Like all great cathedrals, it has many chapels. In a large cathedral, people go from chapel to chapel and finally settle at the place where they feel a special connection with a presence greater than themselves. The cathedral of the great outdoors offers us many chapels. Some people enjoy the mountains; others like the lakes or rivers or streams. Still others prefer the desert (a great gift if you live in Arizona.) God seems to have a preference for the desert. We see in the Old Testament the story of God and His chosen people, how in the desert they were courted and purified. We see in the New Testament men who watched a star appear on a night that changed the world. God had decided to join His creation.

Either/Or vs. Both

In the wilderness, we are spoken to in silence. We are brought to awe and wonder as we gaze at what is offered to us. Wherever there is wonder and awe, a spiritual response has been awakened within us. It is here we have been gifted with the knowledge there is a Presence greater than ourselves. This place has become a holy place for us. These places in Celtic spirituality are called "thin places." That's why there have been many discussions between those who say, "It is only in nature I can meet God," and those who say "it is only in church I meet my God." Why can't it be both rather than either/or? When we get into the either/or battle, we are looking for a winner and expecting a loser. That is religiosity. When we are prepared to accept both, we take up residence in the realm of the spiritual. The spiritual journey is all about accepting both.

Ed Sellner wrote, "My pre-Christian ancestors had a great belief that design pervaded every aspect of life, and that spirits live everywhere in the ancient trees and sacred groves, mountaintops and rock formations, rivers, streams and holy wells. The Celts living close to bodies of water with their dream-like fogs and mists also developed a respect for the mystical. They came to associate water with mystery and personal communal transformations."

Many of us are all familiar with the following words:

"Oh Lord my God, when I in awesome wonder,
Consider all the worlds Thy hands have made;
I see the stars, I hear the rolling thunder,
Thy power throughout the earth displayed.

Then sings my soul, my
Savior God, to Thee,
How great thou art, how
great thou art.

When through the woods,
and forest glades I wander,
and hear the birds sing
sweetly in the trees.

When I look down, from
lofty mountain grandeur
and see the brook, and feel

the gentle breeze
Then sings my soul..."

These words celebrate in our religious experience what has been our experience in the great outdoors. Our liturgy becomes a liturgy with soul because it connects with our everyday experience.

Celebration

"Open our eyes to see your hand at work in the splendor of creation in the beauty of human life. Touched by your hand, our world is holy. Help us to cherish the gifts that surround us; to share your blessings with our sisters and our brothers, and experience the joy of life in your presence."

This was the opening prayer of the Mass I attended during a weekend not too long ago. Having spent a week walking, hiking and driving through God's awesome and mysterious creation, that prayer really said something to me. Prayer is sometimes described as "the outward expression of inward faith." In the above prayer, I found I was presented with a summary of my evolving belief in the wonder-fullness and the awe-fullness that is to be found in the cathedral of the great outdoors. It spoke to me exactly where I was. It brought to mind the moments of my week's journey. It did, as liturgy is supposed to do, connect deeply with my week's experience. As I joined the celebration, I brought that experience into the gathering of the community. My attendance at liturgy that weekend intensified my experience of my daily life.

With the community, I prayed, "Open our eyes to see your hand at work in the splendor of creation." To me, it is expressing my belief that God is at work at this very moment in all of creation. We can see that our world has been created, but do we always accept the fact that it is also still being created? Our world has been shaped and is being shaped. We, too, as human beings, are created, but in each moment of every day we are re-created anew. Humanity and creation are in the process of being perfected. We have a long way to go, obviously, but the process is in place and will not be derailed or denied.

Frustrated?	Yes
Opposed?	Yes
Denied?	Yes
Prevented?	No

That is the great source of hope for us as we face these troubled times.

Chardin in his wonderful essay entitled, *The Mass on the World*, has this wonderful prayer:

"I pray, lay on us those your hands — powerful, considerate, omnipresent, those hands which do not (like our human hands) touch now here, there. But, which plunge into the depths of the totality, present and past, of things so as to reach us simultaneously through all that is most immense and most inward within us and around us."

The creative spirit of God is at work in our world. We have been invited to be "co-creators and co-perfectors of His universe" – a universe where we have been invited to be stewards. It is not our business to possess. We will not take any of its materials with us. As Billy Graham once said, "There is never a U-haul behind a hearse." Each one of us is here for a time to add our own unique shade and color to the tapestry of creation. The more we are in tune with the Creator, and the more effective we are as co-creators, then the more we appreciate our God-given talents as gifts to be gifted in the concrete circumstances in which we find ourselves, always in the here and now. We have been gifted with a great responsibility of serving as good stewards of all the Creator's gifts.

> *"In wilderness is the preservation of the world."*
> — HENRY DAVID THOREAU

I am so impressed at how Native Americans see themselves as stewards of all the gifts of creation, keeping in mind those who are to follow. There is one tribe which, when it comes to decision making, asks the question, "How will this choice affect five generations from now?" The wonderful reverence they show for all of creation and not just some of creation is awe-inspiring.

On the other hand, it is so heartbreaking to see how far we have drifted from the ideal. What a price we are paying. From the 1970's commercial, I still carry with me the image of the Native American with a tear in his eye looking at all the garbage strewn about in nature.

We are being awakened to the reality that we cannot continue to treat nature the way we have been for so many years without suffering the consequences. How glibly we say when someone is diagnosed with cancer, or a baby is born deformed, or a miner has black lung disease, "It is God's will." We are making God the great scapegoat. It is not His will. We are just ignoring His will for His creation. It is not "God's will" to pollute streams, rivers, and underground water supplies with toxins that bring disease, suffering, pain, tragedy and torment. My God is not destructive.

However, many people believe it is good business to keep that god around and well. He adds to the bottom line of companies while at the same time so many innocent men, women, and children find their lives have bottomed out in the prison of powerlessness.

God's hand is at work in our world, and He has called each of us from all of eternity to be His hands, His arms, His eyes, His legs, and His ears. God has called us to be His galvanizing presence to stop the destruction and start the reconstruction, to forge a newer and better understanding of what His creation means, and to deepen our understanding of His plan, not the plans of those whose self-interests are greed, profit, and gain and to heck with the consequences.

❧ Chapter 2: ❧
Rocks & Refuge

I was visiting Steamboat Springs, Colorado and went to the Visitor Center to get advice on good hiking spots. I asked about a trail I had become aware of during a previous visit. On that occasion, I was photographing the waterfall that you see on every Coors can. While I was there, I noticed a trail on the left to another waterfall. A posted sign stated the trail climbed 2,400 feet in a matter of two miles. At the Visitor Center, I asked the young attendant about the difficulty of that climb. I was told the first 1,800 feet was a pretty straight shot with no switchbacks (zig-zag courses within a hiking trail). Then it would level off, and the rest of the climb was not too difficult.

So I began my hike on that trail. It was, understandably, not too, too bad in the beginning. Then it came to mind that when things are going well for us, we can saunter along with not a care in the world. It's only when the going gets tough that we have to slow down and measure each step as we move along. We appreciate each step that we take; we take no one step for granted. Each little step makes that next step possible. In this mode, we move slowly on and on. Up and up we go. (That is a great paradigm for the spiritual journey)

Well, as I went up and up, needless to say I was really suffering. My lungs were aching. Steamboat Springs is located at an elevation of about 10,000 feet above sea level. Several questions then began to enter my mind: "How much longer can I keep this up?" "How much more effort is there in me?" As I looked higher up the trail, I saw a really big rock right in the middle of the trail. I told myself if I can get to that rock, then I can rest and have a chance to catch my breath. I was able to make it to the rock. It had a nice flat surface upon which I could rest. The remainder of the hike was great. It was certainly worth the effort to get there.

As I was enjoying my oats and honey granola bar chased by wonderful cool water, I look around. Instead of looking down the trail, I looked up the trail. I was extremely delighted to see that the trail rose only a very short distance before it got lost over the brow. Then I remembered the words of the person at the Visitor Center, "...the trail levels off." That was the good news I needed. To say the least, I was thrilled! This gave me a much-needed burst of energy and enthusiasm. I was able to continue up that trail. Yes, it did level off. I was able to reach my intended destination.

Was it worth it? Yes, it was!

This is an experience I've thought about many times since that hike. What I had said in the past about looking at something long enough and receiving a deeper insight had certainly been true. We encounter "huge rocks" on the trek we call our spiritual journey. At first we see them as obstacles. Then, as we use them as a resting place, we discover a faithful and invigorating God. This leads us to believe in the truth that our ancestors in faith, the Hebrews, discovered. For them, the word "rock" carries with it the meaning of stability, firmness, and faithfulness. As God was their Rock, we also will come to the realization that the same God is our Rock.

I live on my own. I travel on my own. I most often hike on my own. This affords me a great opportunity to think and to reflect. We may say, "That's good, isn't it?" Well, I have learned over the years that "every blessing is a curse and every curse is a blessing."

Being on one's own is both a blessing and a challenge. And as we grow older, we recognize many more dimensions of both these blessings and challenges. The older we get, the more we find ourselves reflecting on what has happened in our own lives and journeys. As we look back, we get caught up in appreciation, thanksgiving and, of course, guilt and regret. But because of God's grace, these feeling are seasoned with an attitude of gratitude. We develop an attitude of gratitude for what has been given to us over the years. And in time (surprise, surprise), we even become grateful for what has been lost and taken away. This concept has come to me from a recent understanding of the death and resurrection of Jesus Christ. It has come from a newer and deeper understanding of the Paschal Mystery. Death is not an end; it is a beginning of new life and a new way of living.

The feelings of guilt and regret lead to a deeper understanding of God's unconditional love and his gracious mercy. His unconditional love enables us to grow in the recognition of who we really are, not who we would like to be, or whom we are expected to be. All of this is a great process that can't be hurried. God sure moves at His own pace (most often very slowly), but who can question the results. My mother taught me a long time ago that "the mills of God grind very slowly, but they grind very true."

This process also leads us only gradually to accept, and in time, appreciate our powerlessness. The truth of what Fr. Richard Rohr says about "the powerlessness of power and the power of powerlessness" becomes an ever-deepening but a verifiable reality. This powerlessness leads to a greater freedom. And this ever-so-slow process of acceptance guides us to a startling revelation: that we were powerless all along and never really realized or accepted it. We ultimately come to the realization that nothing good has ever happened to us because of our efforts. It always was and will ever be the result of God's grace. What a kick in the head that is.

On closer inspection, what St. Paul said is true in every case, "Of ourselves we can do nothing, but we can do all things in Him that strengthens us."

In Psalm 18, we pray the words, "Who but God is the Rock?"

In Psalm 127: "Unless the Lord builds the house, they labor in vain who build."

In 2 Samuel 22:32: "For who is God except the Lord? And who is a rock save our God?"

There are many, many other references to the wonderful analogy between what a physical rock reveals to us and the reality of who our God, the living God, really is.

On my hike in Steamboat Springs, I remember I did not want to sit on the ground or on a log. I sat on a rock. Sitting on that rock gave me a great sense of security and stability. This was so important when I had exhausted my resources and I needed a boost from outside of myself. We are also told in the Scripture that our God "is our refuge" and "the source of our strength." As I dwelt on the many similarities between the rock and the Rock, I began to understand these Scripture passages more clearly, reflecting on the miracle of grace as a never-ending process.

"An early morning walk is a blessing for the whole day…We must walk like a camel, which is said to be the only beast which ruminates while walking."
— HENRY DAVID THOREAU

The Cocktail

One Sunday morning, I got up and went for a hike in the wonder-full early silence of the morning. There is just something different about the silence of a crisp, bright Sunday that speaks to me in a way other mornings fail to do.

I hiked up Telegraph Pass on South Mountain. When I arrived at the road midway up the mountain, I took a left and continued on the National Trail. That trail is like the mercy of God, (or some might say like one of my sermons) – it goes on and on and on. When I got into the rhythm of the hike, I began to think about what I might encounter that day. Initially, as is often the case, my mind was a blank. Then the prose of Henry David Thoreau came to me: "Me thinks the moment my legs begin to move, my thoughts begin to flow."

I began to think about an incident that occurred in Steamboat Springs a few weeks back. That hike was a very difficult time for me.

After hiking for quite a while, I decided to take a rest on a rather large rock. As I relaxed and collected my breath, some thoughts on what it means to be authentically human and what it takes to be at home in our as yet not fully-redeemed humanity entered my mind. It struck me that these concepts of full humanity are intertwined with the spiritual reality of redemption. Both are real and are interconnected. So how about making a cocktail of the two and let's see what happens.

Warning; this idea may be contrary to some preconceived belief in which we find security. This belief gives us a false sense of security which when lost, leads us to unnecessary pain and turmoil. Thank God this so-called "losing," is in reality the beginning of a newer, deeper, and more life-giving relationship with the Living God.

Pain-full?
Lonely?
Shattering?
Discouraging?
Wonder-full and Liberating?

All these emotions lead to a new way of acting, which in turn, leads to a new way of thinking. These gifts are not to be selfishly hoarded; they are given to us to be shared with others. And it is only in this honest sharing that we realize what has been gifted to us. The sharing experience somehow lessens the pain, and enables us to realize that our suffering was not in vain. This realization is a new wisdom that has been given to us. This wisdom comes to us as we apply our faith to living our everyday life. Wisdom is not the same as knowledge. Wisdom comes with the experience of living in the reality that is grounded in God, in whom we live and move and have our being.

With this wisdom, we go from "wandering wanderers" to "*wondering* wanderers." Through the miracle of grace, we are led from acting as wounded wonders to the miracle of serving as wounded healers. Truly, it is amazing grace that allows us to see the connections among all that is. We ultimately come to the realization that the poverty we are so in dread of is in the reality the rock on which we rest and find peace. Not only is it the rock (surprise, surprise), it's also a net into which we can fall safely to be embraced by our loving Father – God. Now that is a strong drink. It's deadly for the ego; it's encouraging and nourishing for the real, true self. Drink up.

"Our weaknesses become our strengths, the source of our compassion for others and the basis of our awakened nature."
— JOHN HALIFAX

Three Gifts

Before I travel on really long trips, I do a great deal of reading and research. I first decide on the general direction I'd like to go. Taking into account the information I've gathered, I then get down to the specifics of the proposed journey. I bought a book on the great Northwest and promptly left home without it. Oh, these senior moments!!!

But on the other hand, am I not old enough to get away with an occasional senior moment? When I was younger and asked for a room key to replace the one I lost or left in the room, I got dirty looks. Now, thank the Good Lord, I get smiles, or in some cases, sympathetic words. Being a part-time senile senior sure makes life exciting and never dull. Sorry, I digress.

When I get to my hiking location, the first thing I do is head for the Visitor Center. Some centers are very welcoming and treat you very hospitably. You're given the impression they're excited to see you and are anxious to help make your stay enjoyable. In these cases, I find myself looking forward to my stay with added excitement. However, other centers lack that enthusiasm. You can come away with the feeling that the person there sees life as a burden. And your presence and questions add to their burden. Is that not the same feeling we get when we seek information or directions from many church offices?

Those helpful individuals at visitor centers are more than happy to share their experiences of encounters with animals in the park in a particular place. They enjoy telling you about the last time they saw a wolf, a bear, an elk, a moose, and where the encounter occurred. They'll share with you their hiking experiences. They offer tips on what trails to take and what to expect. I always want to know if there are switchbacks. From those discussions, I leave with a greater sense of enthusiasm and confidence. I can also look at my spiritual journey much like a hike.

Just as I have to do my reading and research for my intended hike, I do the same for my spiritual journey. I listen to the experiences of those who have made the journey before me so I'll be better prepared for the challenges that lie ahead.

I read the books written by those who have travelled the trails of their spiritual journey, but reading and researching can only do so much to prepare me for my spiritual expedition. Only in the lived moment – in the existential moment – does the mystery of the time, place, and space really impact us. Here we are often stopped in our tracks and are able to join with St. Peter in saying, "How good it is, Lord, that we are here."

One of my favorite guides for my daily hike is Fr. Ronald Rolheiser's book, *Against An Infinite Horizon.* I see this book as a source of knowledge, leading to a deeper understanding of the spiritual hike I am called to make every day, along the life-trail that's shrouded in the mist of mystery.

On one of my sojourns, I made a rather big mistake. In journaling about blessings, I left out the mutual blessings that couples who are in a relationship need to bestow on one another. I honestly believe that the mutual blessing of those in a relationship will bring an ever-deepening sense of serenity, peace, joy, and love to that relationship. How can this happen you may ask?

Here's what Fr. Ronald has to say: "To bless someone is to speak well of them." But this implies a special form of "speaking well." To bless someone is, through some word, gesture, or ritual, to make that person aware of three things:

1) that after making the earth and humans, God said it was "good, very good;"
2) that God experiences the same delight and pleasure in him or her that the Father experienced with Jesus at His baptism when He said, "This is my beloved child in whom I take delight," and;
3) that s/he who gives the blessing, recognizes that very same goodness and takes that same delight in that person as did the Father.

What a gift our God has given us. We can bless another, and in that blessing we speak a deeper truth. To be blessed is to know we are the Beloved.

"To be unblessed is to be bleeding in a very deep place," writes Fr. Ronald. We can make a difference in the lives of those whom our God places in our life by being His instrument of blessing. What faith our God has in us mortal humans in whom is hidden this MYSTERY.

Shower...of...Shalom

We are afforded the great gift of forty days to prepare ourselves for the great feast of Easter. We celebrate The Paschal Mystery again and again because we are ever experiencing that reality, always anew. So you see, we have to take this year's experience of the mystery and confer on it uniqueness, by celebrating it as a new and never before reality. That is precisely what each and every liturgical celebration is. We take three days to celebrate The Easter mystery, The Paschal mystery. These twenty-four hours are from evening to evening. From the evening of Holy Thursday to the evening of Good Friday is one day, and the same with the other two days. Now we are going to be afforded another 50 days to contemplate how we experience what we celebrated as a daily realty. Otherwise, Jesus Christ did all that he did, suffered what he suffered, for nothing. His life was then a farce, and the same could be said of our lives too.

It is our lives, being led as the life of The Contemporary Christ, that gives our life and every second we lead, untold value. In each and every moment of our lives, in each and every action of our lives, we are revealing anew, Jesus Christ. I live, no not I, it is Christ who lives. What an amazing power grace has, and how Gently is it exercised. This gentleness is portrayed in the first meeting of the Risen Christ with His Dispirited disciples.

What a feeling there must have been in that room. The fear had to be palpable. The doors were locked. They had to speak in whispers for fear of detection. They had to reflect on the events of the Last Supper, Gethsemane, the betrayal by one of their own, the denial by one of their own, the suicide, the scourging, the mockery, the scorn, that long journey to Calvary, the crucifixion, the burial, the closed tomb, now the news of the empty tomb. They had to reflect on their own failure to be a supportive presence. When their Leader needed them most, they were not there. Just a very few were able to stand and be counted, the rest fled in fear. Now, there are the feelings not only of fear, there are feelings of helplessness, confusion, bewilderment, hopelessness, frustration, guilt, disappointment, anger, shame, hurt and pain. As those were the feelings of the disciples, so they are our feelings today. We only have to be honest enough to admit them. Human nature does not change. As it was, so it is, and ever shall be. We, each day have the great challenge of being humble enough to embrace and admit to the human condition.

"We are born human and spend our whole life coming to understand what human means." (J. Metz) An ever deepening reflection on the Paschal Mystery is one of the avenues open to you and me. There are times when we can reflect on this mystery from a distance. Other times life immerses us in a depth we never expected to be in, or in a place we never expected to be. Life throws us some real curve balls, and we are left lost, beaten, bruised and bewildered. We seem to have no way out. We are now ready to encounter the reality of the risen Christ. We are now in the best possible place to receive the gifts He brings. We are lost. We are empty, and emptied out. We are in the best possible place. We are now open to having a Savior. This Savior brings with Him, not peace, but Shalom. Shalom is something much more than peace. The wish for

Shalom brings with it the following. Hold out your emptiness so you can receive the following;

Completeness, wholeness, health, peace, welfare, safety, soundness, tranquility, prosperity, perfectness, fullness, rest, harmony, the absence of agitation and discord.

We think of peace as just the absence of war. The Shalom on The Risen Christ is so much more than that. It is always there for us. Here is a little exercise I recommend. Take a look at that list. Then take a look at your life's journey. Now make a decision about the particular gift you are in need of right now. As you stand under the shower, let the running water be the reality of what you ache for. You will have to leave your shower at some point in time, but let that memory of the running water be a constant reminder of a deeper reality. That reality is GOD pouring down you as constant stream, the gift you so desire. This constant stream will pour down on you each and every second of the day. I must remind you, you are in charge of the faucet. God cannot take over your free will, He loves you too much. God will not turn that faucet for you. I hope and pray you will love yourself enough to enjoy the…Shower…of…Shalom.

Live & Learn

On a hike, there is a great feeling when you're able to see far down the trail. It's even better when you're looking downhill. I was finishing up a hike in Steamboat Springs, Colorado when I heard the cry of someone who was not having a good day. I came around a bend and standing there was a young mother looking down the incline. Her daughter was pushing her bike up the hill, and seemed relaxed about it. However, it was different for her brother. "My son isn't able to ride his bike up the hill, and he is really upset," she explained. He didn't look like a very happy camper as he pushed his bike up the incline. His mother was so positive, but he wasn't ready to listen to her or accept her words of understanding and support. His body language was loud and clear: "I am not listening to you; I am not paying attention to you; just leave me alone." I couldn't help but to think how often we as adults have found ourselves in the same boat? Thank the Good Lord that boat is not the Titanic! But for some unfortunate souls, because of the choices they make, it is the Titanic.

I was finishing my hike, but I wasn't finished with the encounter on the trail. I knew there was a lesson to be learned. And I waited for it to surface. Whatever is REAL for us reveals to us some aspect of the spiritual. In all that is real – all that is perfectly hidden and perfectly revealed – there is the Divine Presence of our God.

We've heard the axiom: "Every picture tells a story." Well, on that hike I was told, and we all have to be continually reminded, that all reality is the ongoing revelation of God. That's the meaning of the expression: "the sacrament of the present moment." So what gift was given to me from that meeting on that hike?

Well, as I've mentioned, I like to compare our spiritual journey to a hike. On the hike of life, we discover what it really means to be spiritual beings wrapped in the oh-so-human condition. On a daily basis, we have to continue to learn – to be taught how not to just exist, not just survive, but to live fully this human journey we call life.

That morning, I began to hike a new trail. Yet, what I encountered was the same struggle that is met in every human endeavor. When we experience an authentic human event, the action of a knowing mind and a consenting will involves both the human and the divine. That is why every, and I really mean every person, place, event, and action is a face-to-face encounter with a new revelation of who my God is for me. Yes, our God is ever new, and at the same time, so ancient. This is a good place to reflect on the words of St. Augustine: "O, Beauty, ever ancient, ever new." These can be our words as well, as we live out each and every new moment in a creation that is ever ancient and ever new.

From all I have read and been told, this Earth of ours has been in existence for about 4.5 billion years. I overheard a park ranger describing some minerals saying what happened 700 million years ago gives us what we have today.

In this world of ours, we discover the very ancient and the ever new. But at any moment in our daily life, we find ourselves in a time and place that never was and never will be again. Each step in this life is a unique step; each life is a life designed by God to be unique. Remember my encounter with the mature couple when I asked them how they were doing? They replied, "Uniquely." In that moment, they were living the reality we are discussing here.

God is not threatened by uniqueness; we are. We want conformity to expectations so we won't be threatened by intimidating surprises. But God always appears in the most unexpected places, and in the most surprising of people. God as a vulnerable baby; God as the betrayed, the broken, the bruised, and the beaten. God is not threatened by what appears to us as a loss. He turns all of our so-called temporal losses into eternal gains.

That young boy who had tantrum on the trail came face-to-face with his limitations. He had to deal with what he was unable to do right then. In time, he would conquer that hill. It may not be the next day or the next week. It would happen on the condition he plays his part. And his part, as with all of us, was to practice in the same way the spiritual life calls us to *practice*.

I pointed out to the young mother that that was a teachable moment on what it means to be human. She could gift her child with a sense of healthy shame – I am human, and I am limited. How many of us were never taught that lesson? We've had to learn it the hard way. Yet there are so many people in denial. We humans want to be perfect. However, this is a physical impossibility. It's not defeat. Rather it's an opportunity afforded to us to journey to acceptance, freedom and the embracing of our limitations.

The good news? We now have a Real Savior God. We also are freed from the burden of perfectionism. We are freed from the bondage of the false self. Consequently, we are given the gift of being able to embrace our faults, our failings, and our disappointments. By embracing our lack of perfection, we are led to the great freedom of being able to live a life of honesty. This is not the hopeless end. On this hike, we're led to a beginning that is ever ancient, ever new. This, of necessity, will enable us – will empower us – to claim our belovedness on a new and ever-deepening level.

Thomas Merton has this to say in his book, *No Man is an Island*: "We must accept the fact that we are not what we would like to be. We must cast off our false, exterior self like the cheap and showy garment that it is. We must find our real self, in all its elemental poverty, but also in its very great and very simple dignity; created to be a child of God capable of loving with something of God's own sincerity and His unselfishness."

❧ Chapter 3: ❧
GPS: God's Persistent Safety Net

I travel a great deal – more than 10,000 miles in 2008. Not bad for a fellow who has no sense of direction! I tell people, "I can get lost in a bathtub." When I want to remember how to make a left turn, I bless myself using my right hand and then go in the opposite direction. When friends express concern about my taking long journeys alone, I reveal the fact that I do have a GPS system.

I believe if you look at life long enough, there is a sermon right there before your eyes. As we take the path of life, a GPS system provides the right direction in which to travel. Since I have trouble knowing which is left or right, I don't always take the correct turn. Then, when I take a right rather than a left turn, or more often miss the turn completely, I hear the word "recalculate." I continue on for a distance in what I think is the right direction only to hear again, "recalculate." There are no other comments like, "Bad move, Dummy. What's wrong with you? Can't you follow directions?" "Are you asleep?" "Don't you understand?" No. Nothing but an unemotional and sterile "recalculate."

The same is true with God. God in His incredibly mysterious love has given us free will. He has also given us the spirit of truth, which when we listen, gives us good orderly directions. In fact, G-O-D can stand for Good-Orderly-Directions. When we take the wrong turn or decide to take a route other than the correct route, God says to you and me, "I will help you recalculate. However, I'm not re-calculating the grace you need for this new situation in your life."

We seem always to be forcing God by our choices in life to recalculate. I have been asked, "How about U-turns?" As a matter of fact, our spiritual journey is all about U-ees! That is exactly what conversion is: turning around and going in the opposite direction. Our self-will leads in one direction. But God's will turns us around to go into the direction of His will. That is always the challenge that goes on between the ego and the true self. The less ego, the less self-centeredness, the less selfishness we have, the less God has to recalculate.

The Father of the Prodigal Son had hopes for his two sons. As you might remember, one of his sons was rebellious and rash; the other was angry and resentful. Both sons changed their father's plans. He had to recalculate. We see at the end of the story that the father did not change his generosity or his faithfulness toward either son. Surprisingly, it is the outward "good son" who is inwardly angry. We have both sons/

daughters within each of us. During the first part of life, we deal with the rebellious and rash son/daughter. In the second half of life, we deal with the angry and resentful son/daughter. The spiritual journey involves becoming reconciled with both of these realities within us, and showing prodigal, reckless, extravagant love to both.

Wherever we find ourselves in life, God is there right beside us not saying, "Another fine mess you've got us into." Rather, He says, "I love you, right here, right now. I will give you whatever you need to get back on the right path. I will give you whatever you need so we can restore our true relationship. Let's get it done, together." I think we need to rename The Parable of the Prodigal Son "God's Recalculation."

Continuous Persistence

God shows no partiality in His love for us, nor the place and time where He meets us and greets us. However, we are partial to how we allow God to meet, greet, and love us. Many times in the course of our lives, we feel our options are taken away. Of course, that's not the case. Many times we surrender our options, and give God only one choice as to where and when He meets and greets us.

Free will is such an awe-full gift. It is full of awe, and is full of wonder, and full of mystery. Free will, like all gifts, carries with it great responsibility. When making decisions, I always have to ask the question, "Will what I am doing challenge God to recalculate?"

Having said all of the above, we can now use GPS as shorthand for God's Persistent Safety Net. How comforting that is to know. There is a persistent safety net always there to catch us when our ego-driven decisions cause us to stray, stumble, and fall. God's Persistent Safety Net is GRACE. It is the intense love of our Father God who is always ready to catch us in His Safety Net of grace and never tires of "recalculating."

God's love for us is personal, passionate, and persistent. It is always offered to us not in the place we'd like to be or where we think we ought to be, but in the unique place we are right now. And being receptive to His grace in that unique moment is how we can reach a new heaven and a new earth. This receptivity is our passing from imperfection to the perfection of receiving God's love and grace. God's Persistent Safety Net reaches each one of us in all of the circumstances of our human journey – in relationships with other human beings, in all of creation, and in the imperfections of our "right now."

Don't feel hopeless. Be hope-full. The world IS being transformed. As Mama Cass Elliot said so many years ago, "There is a new world coming; coming in peace, coming in joy, coming in love."

This new creation is coming; it is happening right now. Our

faith tells us we are part of the creation of this new world. We are co-creators with God of a new world, a new creation that is guaranteed by the resurrection. What we have to do is use our X-ray eyes of faith, our optimistic eyes of faith, to see beyond the obvious to the hidden goodness of God. In other words, to the God hidden, revealed and always ready to recalculate. This is the God of the Good News we must proclaim!

We must take on the responsibility, especially now, of reminding ourselves and others of the inherent good that is in all creation – both seen and unnoticed. We don't need to be informed of this as much as we need to be reminded again and again of whom we are, and who it is that is on our side.

"If God is for us, then who can be against us?"

"With God all things are possible."

We must remember that our Good Shepherd will lead us through our dark valleys. We must be people of memory, constantly reminding ourselves of the fact that we are linked forever, and without cost to us, to God's Persistent Safety Net. We need this reminder to be assured and reassured in spite of what often appears to be evidence to the contrary. We must be a people of hope, proclaiming not only by our words but our actions, what grace we have experienced. We must be a people who by our very demeanor are choosing to live life and live it to the fullest.

> *"The glory of God is the human person fully alive."*
> — ST. IRNAEUS

Alive and responding to all that is. Alive and responding to all that is calling for – no, *demanding* – a response. A response born of faith stronger than fear, breaking through the darkness. Proclaiming for all to hear, "Lord, it is good for us to be here – right now."

We have been created to be fully alive and responsive to all that we encounter – a response born of faith, stronger than fear, breaking through the darkness, proclaiming for all to hear that "it is good for us to be here – right now."

How Many Chances

Some weeks ago, I read a question that was posted online: "I wonder how many times the Prodigal is allowed to return?" This is a great question. Why? Because it forces us to focus not on our understanding of mercy and compassion, but on *God's infinite* mercy and compassion.

The simple answer is there is no limit to the mercy, acceptance, empathy, and generosity of our Father. This understanding came to me from my reading and rereading of Henri Nouwen's book, *The Return of the Prodigal Son*. That book radically changed my understanding of the Sacrament of Reconciliation and what it means to be the Beloved. In his book, Nouwen points out that it is the love of the Father that accepts us as "prodigal" (reckless, wasteful, and uncontrolled). We are the rebellious sons and the resentful sons (or rebellious daughters and resentful daughters). Both rebelliousness and resentfulness are living and at war within each one of us every day. So also is the presence of the forgiving Father. All three dwell within the cave of our souls.

In our rebellion, we leave the home where we are loved with a reckless love. We move to a far-off land. In that far-off land, we seek what we have left behind. But we can never find a home to be "at home" in. Yet, it is in that far-off place away from the comfort of home, in a moment of clarity, which always comes to us in pain, that we are reminded of who we are, where we are, and what we have left behind. So we make a U-ee and head back knowing we will be received as the rebellious offspring, with a reception beyond our expectation and imagination.

The rebellious son just wanted to return home to become one of the hired hands with no expectation of relationship to the family. But the father wanted none of that. He placed his son back into his inheritance, and I'm sure, to the consternation of the resentful son. But the return to his rightful place came with responsibility. The rebellious son will one day have to be like his father. This will take a great deal of hard work, patience, and perseverance. Upon his return home, the prodigal son's plan was to practice evasion. Evasion does not bring out the best in us. And so, the father said "no." He wanted the best for his son, and so he would not allow him to avoid the celebration as the son wished. The father not only wanted everything that is good for his beloved son, but what is BEST for him.

The Father is the incarnation of Paul's words on love: "Love is patient; love is kind; love takes no offense and is not resentful." These qualities of love defined the father. He is patient with his rebellious son. When his son returns, the father asked no questions like, "Why did you do this to me?" or" I gave you so much, but you took your share and wasted it." The love of the father is not resentful; only accepting. As he grows older, the son has a wonderful gift to share with those who will need a love that is patient, kind, and takes no offense.

Here is what the anonymous author of *The Cloud of Unknowing* wrote in the 14th century: "I believe...that our Lord deliberately chooses to work in those who have been habitual sinners rather than in those who by comparison have never grieved Him at all. Yes, He seems to do this very often. For I think He wants us to realize that He is all merciful and all mighty and He is perfectly free to work as He pleases, where He pleases, and when He pleases."

I have read that passage over and over so as to get the full force of its meaning. It's always like a splash of cold water in the Arizona July heat. It cleans, refreshes, and encourages. It strengthens, it vivifies, it frees up something inside. It offers us a new strength, and a new hope. It gives a revived strength for a new phase of the journey to carry on.

What was really amazing to me when I first read *The Cloud of Unknowing* was that the author believes that our God DELIBERATELY chooses those of us who have been habitual sinners rather than the "goody-two-shoes." for special attention. That word "deliberately" really blew me away. It doesn't make sense. God's ways of acting have never made sense to those who see things through this world's lenses. This human confusion is reinforced by what is written in the Scriptures: "His ways are not our ways, and His thoughts are not our thoughts." (I thank God for that. Lucky me).

Over the years I have observed in families how the mischievous child, the one who is always in and out of trouble, will forever claim a special place in a corner of his/her mother's heart. The world may give up; the family may give up; society may give up on us; and perhaps even a church may give up. But a mother's love which is just a manifestation – an incarnation of God's love – NEVER gives up.

Yes, Scriptures tell us even if it were possible for a mother to forget the child of her womb, God cannot and will not ever forget. With His Persistent Safety Net, God is always recalculating what we need, not what we want, in the very place where we are right now. Wherever we go, wherever we stand, wherever we may be, we will always stand on holy ground. The reality of GPS is that His grace is always there for us – reaching out and offering us the right and healthy way. We must continue to fine-tune the ears of our hearts so that we can hear the oh-so gentle voice guiding us safely home. The question is, are we willing to listen?

Staying Alive

In the parable, Jesus does not tell us whether the rebellious son ever stayed. We are never told whether he grew up to be like his father. We never learned whether the resentful son ever went into the celebration for his brother's return. We never learned whether the two sons ever reconciled. (That Reconciliation is a process that takes place – is taking place – within each one of us right now.) Jesus, the wonderful teacher, rabbi, leaves us then with more questions than answers. The spiritual life is virtually always about the question, not about the answer. Why? The answer leads to a new and deeper question. This process goes on and on and on…

Sometimes our electronic GPS systems cannot find a satellite connection, and so we are stranded without any source of good direction. But with the GPS system He provides, the source of our "good orderly direction" lies deep within each of us. It never fails, goes to sleep, loses power, or ceases to function. It has, we could say "a lifetime guarantee."

Our GPS not only provides us with good direction, but also provides us with life, light, and strength for the journey. On top of all of that, (I am now sounding like a TV salesman) "it's free!" No subscription to run out; no renewal notices in the mail; no late charges. It's a gift paid in advance. All we have to do is love ourselves enough to enjoy it.

The Saboteur

As spiritual beings having a human experience, we are not always aware of or prepared to listen to what our GPS is offering us. That is why we need to remember that the power of the Toxic Trinity (guilt, fear, and shame) always stands ready to sabotage the GPS System. When the *saboteur* is effective in disrupting The System, we fall victim to fear, isolation, loneliness, discouragement, and the list goes on and on and on. But it is so very reassuring to know that the recalculating love of our God is always ready to guide us back on track. There is great consolation in the words of the hymn, Hosea: "Come back to me with all your heart, do not let fear keep us apart."

To bring about this return and reconciliation, the ever-present love of God, who is prodigal in His love, is offered to us so we can "live deeply our new life." This new life goes deeper and deeper and deeper. With each departure and return of the rebellious son/daughter, something wonder-full happens. The grace for the return will always be there. Through the mystery of grace, which is beyond our comprehension, the persistent voice calling us "Precious," calling us "Beloved," calling us the "Apple of His eye," will always operate within us. Unfortunately, we are able to ignore the voice, but that does not change the commitment of the voice. It is up to us to open our hearts, hands, souls, and minds to receive the gift.

Many years ago, a popular poster showed a little boy, fully dressed, standing on a junk heap. The caption read: *"I know I'm special since God don't make no junk."* Do we believe that?

The more difficult question is if God doesn't make junk, why on earth do we treat ourselves or allow others to treat us as if we are junk? It's because we listen to the wrong voice. There are dueling voices within us. One voice invites us to live in a world that is sometimes unbelievable. It is a world beyond our imagination where we are living in freedom and the presence of our living God. Then there's the other voice, the voice of the *saboteur*, which doesn't want us to enjoy this wonder-full gift that is freely given.

The saboteur wants to destroy the goodness that is ours. It wants to destroy by every means imaginable all that is healthy, all that is fullness, all that is Holy. Make no mistake; the saboteur has the power to make this happen. But it does not have all the power. The All Powerful One is God. He is on our side and at our side no matter what happens. He tells us "Fear not. I am with you."

"In religion there lurks the fear that we invented the story of God's love."
— SEBASTIAN MOORE

The saboteur seems to have *some* wisdom, but it does not have all wisdom. All wisdom belongs to the Holy Spirit who dwells within us. The saboteur knows *some* of the truth, but it does not know all of the truth. All Truth is its enemy, but our friend. We are defended by this Truth as adopted *chosen* children of God.

As chosen children, we are given the strengthening spirit as our inheritance. It is our inheritance we are invited to enjoy in the *here and now*. When we don't accept that inheritance, what has happened? The voice of the saboteur dominates the airwaves of our hearts, souls, and minds. It is a noise that wants to drown out the voice of Truth that reminds us that "We are the Beloved. We are the Precious. We are the Apple of our God's eyes."

Hell is that place where there is no love. God does not send us to Hell; we choose to journey and dwell in that place of isolation and torment through the exercise of our own free will. We make a choice at every bend in the road, every moment of every day. "It is Heaven all the way to Heaven, and it is Hell all the way to Hell."

The Trash-Talker

I learned to play golf in Ireland. My Dad was my teacher, and a good one. Before I stopped playing, my handicap was in the single digits. (It is not a good sign when a priest's golf handicap is in single figures. It may mean the parish could be suffering). I learned early on that all golfers were not as polite on the course as my Dad. I played a lot with my friends who loved to "bustle" a bit. When I came to America, I found out that expression is translated as "trash-talking." How hard it is to play and concentrate on a game with a trash-talker. The trash-talker's goal is to throw you off your game by distracting you from focusing on what you wish to accomplish; to distract you from the here and now. It is meant to antagonize you, discourage you, disorient you from where you are and from what you are doing.

One of the many disguises of the saboteur is trash-talking. The devil is the foremost trash-talker. He is always scheming and plotting to undermine our true value, our true self-worth, our true foundation, so he can substitute them for what is shaky within. His goal is to substitute that which is really real with what is illusion and unreal. This will lead to our being disconnected from reality. When we are disconnected from reality, we are ultimately disconnected from God. We must always be reminded that God is Reality. In all of our reality, whatever it may be, God is present. He is not present in the trinity of illusions, which is "could," "should," and "would" and all of their minions.

The trash-talker repeats over and over and over again words meant to denigrate us, our families, and all that is near and dear to us. The trash-talker loves to bring up past mistakes and past failures to challenge our confidence in what we are doing right now. The trash-talker is out to sow seeds of fear in our abilities. He needs the challenge of the present moment. The trash-talker shows no mercy until we are broken-down, beaten-down, and destroyed. The trash-talker's goal is to make each of us a victim and to keep us in our victim-hood. But we have a choice to make at the fork in the road.

The Truth-Speaker

We have the choice to tune out the trash-talker and tune into the voice that is always there to remind and to reassure us of our essential and eternal goodness. That quiet voice – if and when we listen – tells us we are loved for who we are, not for what we did or did not do. It is a straightforward voice with no conditions or restrictions; no reservations or limitations. It says, "I love you." It's the voice that reminds us that we are precious.

This gentle voice is neither devious nor deceptive. It is a voice whose source is Life. Consequently, it wants us to live life in a healthy, meaningful way; not a life lived in deception, discouragement, or despair. The trash-talker wants us dead. The voice of Real Truth wants us to live our life fully. This is the voice of *The Truth-Speaker*. The Truth-Speaker, as opposed to the trash-talker, speaks the truth of whom we are, who we have been called to be, and always reminds us of whom has done the calling. The Truth-Speaker speaks essential goodness and the Eternal Truth that lies within each one of us. The trash-talker wants nothing of that!

Choosing A Path

We then have a choice:

- We can be in dialog with The Truth Speaker who is God reminding us of our essential goodness as His beloved son/daughter.

Or

- We can listen to the trash-talker who wishes to denigrate us into a life of Hell.

Unfortunately, our lives are often influenced by people who spread the noisy and distracting voice of the trash-talker. They have become immersed in the trash-talker's message. They blare into our lives the disquieting messages that life is about power, property, and prestige. They tell us if we don't take their warning about property to heart, we will be destined to live in poverty. If we don't strive for a life of prestige, we will then be a "nobody" just taking up space in their world.

We are so fortunate to be offered the voice of The Truth Speaker. He tells us by His words and through His deeds that there is a better way of looking at reality. We are encouraged to look to the reality beyond the perceived. The Truth Speaker encourages us to look for real power, real property, real prestige where we are. We find all of these in places where the trash-talker fears to venture. The Truth Speaker reveals to us that true power will come to us through our powerlessness. He came to us with no property except a broken humanity that he inherited. His humble prestige is based on his being a child of the local carpenter and his wife.

So the battle rages in our souls. Our well-being, our destiny, and our salvation is the prize. Yes, there are two powers – two forces at war, but the strength of the forces are not equal. God's power is *all* power. And this is the source of our immeasurable hope. It offers us the hope we need to face the force that destroys our lives and wants us dead. The choice is now ours – life or death, hope or despair, freedom or fear.

In order for the saboteur to be successful, he must be devious, a distorter, a detractor, devoid of mercy, a master of disguise, and most of all, a deceiver. Its language is "cunning, baffling, powerful, insidious, and patient." The Scriptures warn that "the angels of darkness appear to us as angels of light," and that every vice is a virtue taken to extremes.

But God will never allow us to be tested beyond our strength. And our strength is the active presence of the love of the infinite God – our God who is always there for us, with us, and within us.

We must pray for the faith to believe that whatever the saboteur does through all of his disguises, it will never, and I mean never, have the power to overcome or overpower us. We are on God's team, strengthened with His spirit, and we shall overcome whatever obstacles the saboteur may place before us.

Yes! God and I can! We can, not I can. It is a WE job!

❊ Chapter 4: ❊
A Question of Time

Many years ago, I was told that to question was to care. People question in classrooms, question relationships, question that which has meaning and significance to them. And so it stands to reason that we will have deep, deep questions concerning the Unknowable and the Indefinable God.

In this time of uncertainty, there is one radical step I encourage each of us to take on a very regular basis. As a matter of fact, this step should be taken many, many times each day. We must claim the words of the Father spoken to His Son at the River Jordan: "This is my beloved in whom I am well pleased." Heather and Tina, you are my beloved daughters in whom I am well pleased. Sean and Peter, open your heart to hear that you are my beloved sons in whom I am well pleased.

This statement is the same for all of us. Each of us is loved by God, even before we were born. Psalm 109 states: "From the womb, before the morning star, have I begotten you." From eternity, you have been loved with an unconditional, unlimited, unrestricted, everlasting love, which by its very nature will be without end. It is now and forever will be eternal love. Over the years, I have given the following quotation from Thomas Merton to many, many teens and those in their early 20s as well as those in their 30s and 40s.

"God, I have no idea where I am going. I don't see the road ahead of me. I can't know for certain where it will end. Nor do I really know myself, and the fact that I think I am following Your will does not mean that I am actually doing so. But, I believe that the desire to please You does in fact please You. And I hope that I have that desire in all that I do. I hope that I will never do anything apart from that desire. And I know that as I do this, you will lead me by the right road though I may not be aware of it. Therefore, I will trust You always, though I may seem to be lost in the shadow of death. I will not fear, for You are ever with me. And You will never leave me to face my perils alone."

Confusion is a necessary part of the journey of life for an authentic human being. God has created us in His image and His likeness, endowing us with an intellect and a will. Since God has given us such great gifts, He definitely wants us to use those gifts. So, go ahead and ask the questions; let questioning be part of your life, and you will be surprised at how gently you will be given the answers.

We live in *kairos* time, not *chronos* time. From my own experience, I struggled with a question for seven years before the answer was revealed in and through my everyday life experience. As I struggled, it dawned on me what my mother had experienced. She told me how she prayed for seven years before a situation revealed itself. There is something about seven I have come to appreciate. In America, people change homes every seven years. Every seven years, many people change jobs. And we are told that every seven years, we ask a new set of questions because the old answers just don't satisfy us anymore.

I have come to realize over the years how God uses time, places, people, and events of our everyday life to reveal His loving and caring. I've come to appreciate that He isn't an indifferent, detached God locked away on His Heavenly throne, but a God who is always present in us and with us (Emmanuel), and He uses our reality to become a reality in our world. We are in partnership with God in the ongoing creation of this world that is entrusted to our care.

Sometimes we recognize this wonderful mystery of God cooperating with us, and the necessity of us cooperating with God to create what He intends. When we have doubts about our abilities and our usefulness in this life, it is then when we are most effective. That's because we know that ultimately, whatever we accomplish for good, it is the creative love of God, the Holy Spirit, who is at work within us, and we are the instruments of His co-creation.

Hanging on...in Faith

Pope John XXIII once said, "We are not on Earth as museum keepers, but to cultivate a flourishing garden."

A positive response to the words of Henri Nouwen: "I am the beloved," will help us cultivate a colorful, vibrant, vital, verdant garden." This very simple sentence is life changing. When internalized and digested, you will find yourself being led to the understanding that God's love is not just an idea or concept; rather, His love becomes for us a "lived experience."

Nouwen prays, "O, Lord, We can only love each other because You have loved us first. Let us know that first love so we can see all human love as a reflection of a greater love; a love without condition or limitation." (*Our First Love*)

We can sometimes see this love exemplified between some married couples. Their love is their constant calling. It reminds us of Our First Love, the love from where we originated; the love we are aching to return to.

The great challenge for us then is to love as we have been loved by God. But we feel we are always coming up short. We are not divine; we are human, and by nature, we are limited. To love as we have first been loved, we must be connected to that First Love. When we either avoid or deny ourselves this Source of Life, we shouldn't be surprised when we find our lives empty, disconnected, lifeless, and off track. We are then left to depend on second love, which by its very nature cannot do what The First Love has done. The memory of The First Love is always with us. It cannot be replaced no matter how hard we may try. To expect that it can be replaced is to court disaster. We have all gone down that path, and the result is addiction, alienation, discouragement, and an entrance into many, many other places of darkness.

Does this sound pretty bleak? Sure it does. But this is where the great gift of faith comes in. We have to learn that what we may perceive as faith is not true faith until and unless it is the only thing we have to hang on to. We have to learn to pray, when our world has crumbled or is beginning to crumble, that God doesn't intend for this to happen. He will take the rubble of our lives, and through His power and our cooperation, He gives to us whatever we need to build our world up again.

I believe Lord. Give me greater faith in You.

Receiving to Give

On June 8, 2011, I was lucky enough to celebrate 48 years in this priest's life that I have been living since age 23. As I mark different milestones, I find myself, like most people, reflecting on what has happened and what is happening right now. We may well ask, "How about the future?" Well, at least for me, the struggle of the present – when my get up and go has got up and gone – is more than enough challenge for me. When we get old, there is a hidden blessing. Because the energy is not there anymore, you have to make "surviving the present moment" your top priority. "Just this moment, Lord, just this moment," is my prayer.

It is great to have no big plans on the horizon; just today; just this moment. I find there is wonderful freedom in that mindset. Not much fodder for the ego. As a matter of fact, there is no food for the ego. That makes the ego a very unhappy camper. And when the ego is unhappy, there is trouble on the horizon. However, in the meantime, there is rest, peace, an appreciation of quiet, and an occasional sense of serenity. Maturing has its blessings.

Don't get me wrong. I still have moments of anger, wild dreams for the future, and grandiosity, just to name a few. But a real good dose of Chronic Fatigue Syndrome acts to blow those thoughts and plans to you-know-where. I have made the following words of a Gaelic song more my own each day: "The cares of tomorrow must wait 'till this day is done."

Serious change has become an obvious reality for me.

The thought of change is now ever before me. Change has to do with loss and gain. These days, that which has been lost can be more easily seen and felt. All I have to do is say two Masses in a row, eat after 5:00 pm, and look in the mirror. Then I become well aware that this body of mine has suffered a loss.

What has been gained is much more difficult to decipher. The gain that replaces the loss is not often seen in a mirror. It appears in moments of reflection. It appears as we reflect in the wonder-full ordinary moments of our not-so-ordinary lives. As we well know, there's no such thing as an ordinary life. There is always the divine wanting to break through so as to say to us, "We are God's living story, right now." But some peoples' present lives is the only story they will ever get to read. That's how much confidence God places in each human being. He must know something we have yet to discover.

Compassion

I was reflecting on this question: "What is the one word that has become a life-changing word for me over the last 48 years?" That word has to be COMPASSION. Over the last 48 years, I have passed through the evolution of the meaning of "church," and have discovered a new and more challenging reality of it. I had to live (no; scratch that. I had to survive) through that liminal space where one reality is replaced with another. It was a time of upheaval. For those who lived through the 1960s and 1970s, you know what I'm talking about.

We had the Vietnam War, the drug culture – everything was questioned. And to top it off, we didn't think we were going to live past 30. That was a blessing because there was nobody over 30 who could be trusted. There was radical change taking place both inside and outside the church. It wasn't an easy time!

We went from the objective to the subjective. Each person's story was the story of God, and so each demanded reverence. There were no longer any glib answers from the textbook. Each person had to be heard … with compassion.

Where did that compassion come from? I was on the receiving end of compassion from many people who were both inside and outside of the church community. There were compassionate people who afforded me a place to bring my weary and sometimes broken being where I could rest for a while. These people were not there to fix me; they were there to listen to me, and when necessary, suffer with me. This is the true meaning of compassion. I was then able to move on, and in some cases, struggle on, renewed in spirit.

Looking back, I can say from experience that no place compares to that kind of sanctuary where we can freely express our anxiety and fears, reveal who we really are, and not be judged or condemned. That was a sacred place to bring the harsh judgments; the unrealized, impossible, broken dreams; and to be received with tender care and a life-giving love. My black-and-white life took on many shades of gray. I can now look back and see the truth in the words, "Life is not a problem to be solved; it's a mystery to be lived."

Because of my own life's story, I am led to believe that to live the life our God wants us to live, we must immerse ourselves in the mystery of compassion. My list of compassionate fellow travelers is long, and I add to it all the time. The older we get, the more compassion we need to receive. The blessing that comes with that is that we have more compassion to share. We all need compassion to become the person our God intends us to be. In our moments of pain, we don't want glib answers; we want the presence of a real human being; a person who says to us, "I do not have any answers, but I'm here for you. It's going to be okay."

That's about the best thing a human being could ever hope for. So to realize our God's dream for us, The *Aisling* of God, as spiritual beings having a human experience, we need – no, we demand – a great deal of compassion.

Blind Alley

There are great challenges presented to us in the Scriptures. During Mass, it's the job of Scripture readings to deepen our understanding of what it means to be a disciple of Jesus Christ. That challenge comes to us from "The Table of The Word". The strength to face this challenge comes from "The Table of The Eucharist." The two Tables complement one another. We need both to lead a truly Christian life and an authentic spiritual life.

In Isaiah, we are encouraged to..."share your bread with the hungry, shelter the oppressed and the homeless, clothe the naked, and not turn your back on your own." Now if that isn't enough, the prophet goes on to speak as the voice God, "Remove from your midst oppression, false accusation, and malicious speech." We may well say, "This is hard work," and we're correct. The spiritual journey – the spiritual hike – IS a difficult climb. That's why we can't journey alone. Alone, we will be destroyed.

The spiritual journey is a difficult, ego-busting path. We're led on a journey into who we really are as authentic human beings. We're led to that place where we have to honestly face who we are in our limitedness and our brokenness. Until we accept the reality of that place, we will *not* have our Rock of Real Faith to rest and rely on. We'll live in the fantasy world of self-reliance. We will be relying on the world outside of us that doesn't reflect our inner reality. The absolute dependence on God comes to us slowly and painfully, and enables us to embrace all that we face. This Sustaining Force, which is essential for us to live life to the fullest, provides the resources for us to rest and rely upon. This is the essence of Spirituality which is the opposite of the fantasy world of self-reliance (religiosity).

To blast us out of that cozy place, we will have to face some shattering event that rocks us to our core. The old trite answers don't work for us anymore. We now have new questions for which new answers must be found. We get to a place which Karl Rahner calls "a blind alley." This "blind alley" isn't what it appears to be. In reality, it's a new, deeper, and quite different understanding of God. It's a new understanding coming to us in a way that we least expect or could plan to achieve given the choice.

In this blind alley, we find ourselves visiting "the valley of tears and fears." Again and again, we shed both physical and emotional tears. But we must always keep before our mind's eye the wonder-full words: "…in His mercy and love, He allows no tear to go unheeded." There are no tissue moments with God. Nothing is disconnected from the bigger story. There are no garbage cans in The Kingdom. All of our tears are received by God and returned to us as pearls of wisdom, not for ourselves or for religiosity, but for the hungry, the thirsty, the prisoner, the homeless, the immigrant, the traveler, or whoever is the "least of the brethren" you encounter in your daily life. St. Paul reminds us as that "what we have been given is NOT for ourselves but for the building up of the common good."

I have found the following words of Fr. Adrian van Kaam, C.S.Sp. to be both comforting and challenging. These words are from his book, *On Being Involved*.

"Religion and life are not separated. My daily task and its religious meaning, my worldly and religious commitments sustain one another. I can encounter God in the realities of daily life and face all events. (In Him, we live and move and have our being.)

A commitment to God that excludes a commitment to the world will lead to a false religiosity. In a make-believe religious commitment, spirituality may degenerate into an egotistic search for sentiments and fantasies. A split spirit of religious sentiment and imagination can be maintained only when I withdraw emotionally from my commitments. I tell myself foolishly that as soon I get involved in my study and in the people for whom I care, then I have to leave behind that sweet world of religious dreams and sentiments in which I want to indulge.

If, with God's grace, I find the courage to give up this self-centered world of religious sentiment, I may be able to develop a true spiritual life. I may find God where He is: in the needy people around me, in the difficult hours of exhausting study, in the collaboration with humankind for the building of a better world. I find Him in the asceticism of the laboratory where I dedicate myself, together with my brothers and sisters of the human race, to discovery of the concrete scientific aspects of the truth of His creation."

Toxic Shame

We need a constant reminder of Henri Nouwen's great words of consolation in *A Cry for Mercy*, "God's mercy is greater than our sins. There is an awareness of sin that does not lead to God but to self-preoccupation. Our temptation is to be so impressed by our sins and our failings and so overwhelmed by our lack of generosity that we get stuck in a paralyzing guilt."

I believe Nouwen is speaking here about the third aspect of the "toxic trinity," which is shame. Healthy shame says, "I am human, I am limited, I make mistakes and it is okay. I do not have to be perfect." Toxic shame on the other hand takes away the following five rights, which must be reclaimed.

I MUST reclaim the Right to:

Love – which means I do not have to earn, deserve or qualify for love, otherwise, it is not a gift.
Be loved [the beloved] – I am the beloved when I am loved as I am right now. I am loved with a love that is unconditioned, unlimited and unrestricted. It is now and forever. Being the beloved cancels out the need for and the demands of perfection.
Belong – I have always belonged to God's love. The fact that I am living means God's love is supporting me and I will return to the same eternal love. I always belong to the family of Father, Son and Holy Spirit.
Worth-whileness – My right to live fully human life. "The glory of God is the human person fully alive." My worth-whileness is not dependent on what I do, but who I am. "My being proclaimed the greatness of the Lord." As Mary says in the Magnificat.
Have fun [play] – Unless I play, my prayer does not work.

45

We are not born with toxic shame; we are "gifted" with this starting at about age 18-months. We must spend our whole life giving back that toxic gift so we can live God's dream for us on a daily basis. Toxic shame comes to us in words and in phrases. Words like dumb or stupid or phrases like I am ashamed of you, how could you be so dumb, I am sorry you were ever been born... and the list goes on and on. It also comes to us as the result of physical, spiritual, sexual or psychological abuse.

Behind every addiction and compulsion is toxic shame. Behind all of our medicators - abuse of alcohol, drugs, sex, food, shopping, work, gambling, TV, internet, pornography, cutting - is toxic shame. We are blessed to have such wonderful support groups such as Alcoholics Anonymous, Narcotics Anonymous, Gamblers Anonymous, Sex Anonymous, Overeaters Anonymous, etc. etc., which offer to the addict a way out of the addiction into a new way of living an authentic human life. These groups offer the essence of spirituality. They are great examples of how the place of the wound becomes the place of the gift. Those previously wounded now become empowered to be healers from their own experience. When we are in a shame attack, with feelings of not being good enough, or not being deserving, we lose sight of who we are as a beloved son or beloved daughter. A classic example of a shame attack is "poor me." The natural consequences of this will be unhealthy behaviors like those mentioned above.

Toxic Shame wants to kill you and me. Many people surrender to the end consequence of toxic shame and commit suicide. Suicide can be either fast or slow. Toxic shame is terminal, it is death-dealing. This is because toxic shame and healthy spirituality are mutually exclusive. This is not so with religiosity. We are told that religiosity is for those who are afraid of going to hell. Spirituality is for those who have been to hell. Spirituality is the key which unlocks the door allowing one to cross the threshold of shame into a life of peace, joy and love. Every encounter with toxic shame will either strengthen and reinforce a belief in essential goodness or weaken the boundary of belonging.

Religiosity and toxic shame seem to be able to coexist. We will do everything we can to look good on the outside, while actually in a living hell on the inside. The thinking is that as long as the outside practice is okay and I am looking good doing it then I must be okay. Not so. How often have you heard? "The cleaner the house, the sicker the family." or "A clean desk is the sign of a sick mind."

How often do we as individuals, as couples, as families, as parishes, as church, as country, project one thing while we know deep down it is not the truth? We are living a lie. We have a secret. There will always be a secret we are not allowed to speak or share in any way. A secret because of our misbegotten love and we take it to the grave rather than face reality and bring it into the light. Our unhappiness will somehow be connected to our share in the family secret. When toxic shame paralyzes us into inactivity, we are unable to move, we are frozen in place. Something may then happen which will force us to deal with the toxic shame of the secret. This is a moment of conflict. Will I continue to live the life of the lie or grasp onto the outstretched hand of unconditioned, unrestricted, unlimited love which will lead me to freedom? This freedom can be summed up in a new way of living, which comes to us from a new way of acting.

The antidote to toxic shame is a healthy spirituality. Healthy shame, healthy spirituality is always reminding us that we are the beloved, we are loved without conditions or restrictions. We do not have to earn love, deserve love or qualify for love. Love is always being gifted to us without price. We cannot earn what we already have. Unhealthy thinking and unhealthy messages from the family secret will lead us to perfectionism, which according to John Bradshaw is a disease, not a quality to be desired. Those of us who desire to be perfect are usually angry, resentful and short-tempered. Why? Simply because when we want to be perfect we are chasing an illusion. We cannot be what we expect to be or want to be or other people tell us we ought to be. We are never good enough. This in turn will lead us to another visit to the pity-pot, to "poor me." When enough of us get together who are on our pity-pots, we have a pity-party which will only reinforce our sense of powerlessness and alienation. The opposite of this is asking the question, "What am I going to do for me, right now?" You switch the focus from poor me to that of empowerment. We make the choice of being a victim or a survivor. Healthy spirituality is saying to us - by the grace of God, I am who I am right now (St. Paul). Right now I am loved by God. I am being graced. Because I am loved by God right now, I have to make a choice whether I will respond to God's love or choose self-hatred, leading to self-punishment.

Spirituality enables us to become comfortable with being a human being rather than a human doer. When we are authentically human we realize we are in the process of becoming through the actions of God's grace. We are in the process of being born. We are always in the process of giving birth to whom we are.

I find great consolation in the parable of the wheat and weeds. In this parable the servants want to pull up the weeds, but the wise king says, "Let them grow together until harvest time because in pulling up the weeds, you may pull up the wheat as well." As they spring from the earth, the wheat, and in this particular case the weed darnel look very similar. The king is wise because what the servants thought were weeds would have actually been wheat, and what was wheat would have been weeds. This is our spiritual journey. This is the process we go through. What I thought were the strengths of my twenties are now the weaknesses of my sixties. What I thought were the weaknesses of my twenties are now the source of strength for the sixties. Thomas Merton encourages us with these words in *The Gospel of Thomas*, "Be who you already are." We have been loved by our God from all eternity. We are loved right now with the same eternal love we have had from the beginning of time. We will return to that infinite eternal love when our time here is ended. Where that love resides is the heart. The heart in each one of us has never said no to God. I do not care where you have been or what you have done, there is that place in you that has never said no to God. In that place, the Father, Son and Holy Spirit are having a great celebration. There is always an open invitation for us to celebrate. We have been given the freedom to say yes and to say no. When we are living the true life of the beloved, we are open to join in the celebration.

When we are in toxic shame, we do not believe we are good enough or that we have the right to celebrate because we have not earned it, deserve it or somehow in our misguided (diseased) thinking qualify for the celebration. In each moment the decision is made to choose to live life, and live it to the fullest (spirituality) or surrender to death (toxic shame).

There is a great prayer called the Serenity Prayer: "God grant me the serenity to accept the things I cannot change, the courage to change the things I can, and the wisdom to know the difference."

Everybody is familiar with those lines, but not many people know the next two lines: "Living one day at a time, Enjoying one moment at a time."

And that moment is now.

There is No…Other…Way…to Meet God except in the **NOW**.

Scripture tells us, "Now is the acceptable time, now is the time of salvation." In this NOW moment, we make a decision whether to listen to the truth that we are the beloved, or listen to the lie, which is that we are not good enough. In this moment, God is saying to each one of us, "I love you with an everlasting love. It is my gift to you."

From Fear to the Freedom of Faith

In our journey in faith, there are no mistakes. God takes all of our so-called mistakes and compensates for what is missing with His transforming and transfiguring grace. This new creation of grace is gifted

48

back to us, resulting in a new understanding and a new compassion. "Behold, I make all things new," says our God. He does not make new things. This past summer I was on a hike in Colorado for what seemed to be a long, long time. I met no one along the trail. Then I saw three people approaching me. When they saw me, they began to smile and one of them said, "Oh we were beginning to think this was an abandoned trail." None of us wants to hike an abandoned trail. It could mean there is some danger, otherwise it would not be abandoned. You and I are on a trail which is not abandoned, rather we are on the trail to abandonment. Being on this trail is the scariest experience of the many we suffer on our human journey. Many of us are afraid of being alone, being left behind by our friends, being deserted by those who once said they loved us, cared for us and said they would never leave us. On the other hand, how many times will we hang onto to dysfunctional relationships because we are afraid of letting go? We are afraid of a future devoid of a presence we have gotten used to and are afraid to do without. We have to deal with these issues because of our experience with abandonment.

To identify with us and our issues of abandonment, God has sent His son to journey to the place of abandonment, so that when we find ourselves in that desolate place, our God is there to meet us, embrace us, encourage us and strengthen us. Jesus on the cross uttered the searing, agonizing words, "My God, my God, why have you abandoned me?" In the Gospel of Mark, Jesus dies having uttered those words and we have no answer in Mark's Gospel to the question. Even in His Gethsemane moments, Jesus was able to pray to the Father that the cup He was about to drink from would pass from Him. On the cross of abandonment, there is no such Presence, there is no such relationship to call on, and so we cry out the prayer of abandonment.

Over the years, I have come across many individuals abandoned by their fathers and their mothers. The sad fact was that there were two people in the house, a man and a woman, but they were not parents, there were no parents in the home. Thank God there is a great amount of literature and counseling available on the issues of abandonment. In particular, literature for daughters without mothers. Because giving birth to a person does not necessarily mean they are a mother to that person. You can have a man in the house so caught up in work addiction that there is no nurturing time for the life entrusted to him to be cared for and nourished. Abandonment issues result in people who fear letting go. And as a result I have come across people who will stay in dysfunctional relationships long after the realization that they are in an unhealthy environment.

The opposite of fear is faith. When we have issues of fear and anxiety, the scripture offers us words of supplication. Out of the mouth of the Psalmist come these words:

> "Out of the depths I cry unto you oh Lord, Lord hear my prayer.
> Oh God, come to my aid. Oh Lord, make haste to help me."

From the mouth the crucified emptied Jesus: "Father into your hands I commend my spirit."

We then have these words of consolation, "the Lord is close to the broken-hearted and from all their distress He rescues them."

True intimacy with God will only be real when we walk through raw, naked fear. You know from your own experience that real intimacy comes when you leave fear behind and you reveal yourself to another person as you really are, knowing that they love you and accept you just as you are right now. I strongly recommend that wonderful little story "The Velveteen Rabbit." Skin Horse has gifted us these wonderful words, "You are not really real until somebody really loves you."

> "When love awakens in your life, in the night of your heart, it is like the dawn awakening within you. Where before there was anonymity, now there is intimacy; where before there was fear, there is courage; where before there was awkwardness, now there is a rhythm of grace and gracefulness; where before you were jagged, you are now elegant and in rhythm with yourself. When love awakens in your life, it is like a rebirth, a new beginning. The human body is born complete in one moment, but the birth of the human heart is an ongoing process. It is being birthed in every experience of your life. Everything that happens to you has the potential to deepen you." Patrick Kavanagh

> *"Praise, praise, praise*
> *The way it happened and the way it is."*
> —ANAM CARA

This trusting faith is what builds within each one of us from many journeys into the realm of fear. There is an old song "Put your hand in the hand of the man from Galilee."

Allow me to relate two instances which happened on my own journey. In my younger days I used to love to take the kids to Disneyland. One year I was on the paddle steamer looking out across the water. I felt a hand reach into my hand. I looked down and saw two eyes looking up at me. I didn't recognize those two eyes and they didn't recognize my two eyes. So the hand was withdrawn and the kid ran away - hopefully to his parents. Another year at Mass a little girl was sitting next to me.

When it came time for the Our Father, she put out her hand and clasped mine. Then after a little while, she withdrew her hand, picked up her little doll, extended one of the doll's arms to me and kept the other arm linked to her and we completed the Our Father that way. The little girl, the doll and I prayed together. I have never had the same feeling praying the Our Father, either before or since.

There are two choices we can make. We can either hold onto the hand of God or withdraw and run away in fear. Prayer is always an act of presenting ourselves to God as we are and entrusting all of ourselves, the good and the bad, the successes and the failures, the joys and the sorrows - entrusting them into the caring hand of Our Father who is Our God.

For a real, trusting faith, a deepening of honesty is required. To journey from our fears of abandonment to trusting faith, we must be reassured and reassure ourselves that our God meets us, greets us and loves us just as we are. Both faith and love demand trust.

The season of Lent is a season into progressive honesty. It is forty days and forty nights. One evening I was speaking to kids in prison and I mentioned how Lent is for forty days. One young person piped up with "It is forty nights as well." When I said to her, "It is the nights that are the toughest," all she was able to do was nod her head in agreement. It is within darkness, especially the darkness of the night that our greatest fears surface and haunt us. It is then we encounter the wild beasts of our own personal demons. It is in the darkness that the wild beasts of guilt, fear and shame seem to roam at will, resulting in a night of tossing and turning, a night of restlessness and turmoil. Lucky for us, God has given us Psalm 23 where He reminds us He is our shepherd and the dark valley will hold no fear for us. It is also helpful to repeat, "I believe Lord, help my unbelief, I believe Lord, help my disbelief." "Do not be afraid" appears in scripture 365 times. I wonder why our God in His infinite wisdom and mercy would want to remind us of this fact over and over and over again. On our journey through life we have to deal with the uncertainties of life. All we have is right now, this moment - with the rest, there is no guarantee. We do, however, have the guarantee there is no moment our God will not journey in us and through us and with us. No matter what we feel, no matter what we think, no matter what we are told, our God does not and can not abandon us. "He has to be faithful to us because He has to be faithful to Himself." He loves us not because we are good, He loves us because He is good. A belief in His love is an act of faith which will enable us to live life and live it to the fullest.

Yes, His eyes are watching through the lens of His love for us.

Yes, His ears are listening ever attentive to the outcry for His love.

Yes, His lips are speaking, "I love you, you are mine."
Yes, He is our friend ever by our side,
Yes, we are His beloved,
Yes, He is our lover.

Fear knocked at the door. When faith answered, there was nobody there.

Reconciliation and Guilt

When I was preparing for my first reconciliation, I vividly remember being in the old fashioned black box, practicing for the real thing. I must have said something, I can't remember, when a hand came out of that little screen and slapped me across the face, not once, but twice. I ducked the third time! That memory has been with me all of these years. I also remember being invited to a parish to celebrate First Reconciliation with the little ones. I had pulled back the old screen. There was dead silence until I heard a little tinkle and I knew there was no fountain in that reconciliation box. I just cannot imagine the fear in that little person so many years ago.

Over the years we have come to an ever deepened understanding of the Sacrament of Reconciliation. It is not a place we go to receive a slap in the face or to approach with fear, it is an encounter with the loving presence of a God who loves us and accepts us beyond our wildest dreams. His mercy is greater than our sin. It is a mercy we need to experience again and again. Why? Because it is the Sacrament of Reconciliation, not obliteration. Jesus Christ is the only spiritual leader who encourages us to love our enemy. And the enemy is within each one of us. There are some sinful practices that are removed by God's grace, while others remain. It is so encouraging to read what happened to Paul when he had a thorn in his flesh. Because of his fallen understanding he wanted it removed and removed immediately. It did not happen. When he complained to God about the thorn remaining in his life, he heard the words, "My grace is sufficient for you, it is in weakness my power is made perfect." Paul's great response to this was, "It is only when I am weak, and it is then that I am strong." When we go to encounter the gentleness and compassion of God in this sacrament of peace, we are going to confess our need to encounter a God of mercy. "Confession is the part we hate the most." (Richard Rohr) This is a wonderful, freeing understanding of the sacrament that today is so unused, not visited.

The season of Lent has always been associated with penance and the Sacrament of Reconciliation. The journey into our own deserts reveals to us the aspects of our lives for which we need reconciliation with the ministering of angels. This encounter offers each one of us a revelation of God's love for us - our savior Jesus Christ. This is what conversion means - to return, to turn around and return to the always open embrace of our God.

A repentance means returning so we can become truly ourselves.

Turning around to be embraced, so we can embrace who we really are.

Turning around so we can turn our back on guilt, fear and shame.

Turning around so we can be embraced as the beloved.

Let us turn around so we can be who we already are.

Turning around so we can be free from the prison of the lie, so we can be free to live in the freedom of the Truth.

God's truth speaks to us always in the present and this present of God is what we call now.

Toxic Trinity

Our God will never allow us to face a challenge alone, unless of course we exercise our God-given free will and reject, turn our back on his grace, help and love. It is essential we keep before us the great gifts offered to us, to strengthen us to face the challenge of here and now living. Celtic spirituality offers us some wonderful prayers that can be strength for our journey. The first is from Lorica - known as "The Deer's Cry"attributed to St. Patrick,

I arise to-day.
Through a mighty strength,
The invocation of the trinity
Through belief in the threeness
through confession of the oneness
of the Creator of Creation
I arise to-day
through God's strength to pilot me;
God's might to uphold me,
God's wisdom to guide me,
God's eye to look before me,
God's ear to hear to me,
God's word to speak for me,
God's hand to guard me,
God's way to lie before me,
God's shield to protect me.

Another prayer I like; from the Liturgy of the Hours

Your eyes are watchful,
your ears are listening,

your lips are speaking,
friend at my side.

With all of that upper-most in our minds, we can now journey into the territory of the toxic trinity - guilt, fear and shame. This week, we will take a look at guilt, which Erma Bombeck said, "Is a gift that keeps on giving."

Healthy guilt enables us to say, "I made a mistake and I need to make amends, I need to change this behavior." There is also the guilt we hang onto - never forgetting, never forgiving. It becomes a toxic presence in our spiritual life. We are told that our Jewish brothers and sisters discovered guilt, but Catholics perfected it. I am sorry to say there was a huge assist given in this effort by the Irish monks. John O'Donohoe in his book, *Eternal Echoes* has written the following; please read it slowly and reflectively:

> "Sometimes, we feel guilty about things in the past that should hold no guilt for us. Because we feel bad about something, *we exaggerate our part in it* and retrospectively *ascribe more power and freedom to ourselves* than we actually had in the actual situation."

Guilt belongs to the past and the past is over and gone. We have the consoling words from Psalm 103, "As far as the East is from the West, so far have I put your sins behind you." Do we believe God or not? "When personal guilt in relation to a past event becomes a continuous cloud over your life, you are locked in a mental prison. You have become your own jailer." Although you should never erase your responsibility for the past, when you make your past your jailer you destroy your future. It is such a great moment of liberation when you begin to forgive yourself, let the burden go and walk out into a new path of promise and possibility. Self-compassion is a wonderful gift to give to yourself. You should never reduce the mystery and expanse of your presence to a haunted fixation with something that you did or you did not do." John O'Donohoe, *Eternal Echoes*

To learn the art of integrating your faults is to begin a journey of healing on which you will regain your poise and find new creativity. You soul is more immense than any one moment or event in your past. When you allow guilt to fester and reduce you like this, it has little to do with guilt. The guilt is only an uncomfortable but convenient excuse for your fear of growth. Guilt then has to do with self-forgiveness. In the Sacrament of Reconciliation I have come across many people who have never forgiven themselves. They have placed themselves in the prison of guilt and shame. Guilt is "I made a mistake and I need to change and in some cases make amends," shame is "I am a mistake and I need to be punished." Pride is when we do not want to forgive ourselves. We have pride in the fact that somehow our sin is too big for God's love, his compassion and his forgiveness. We are told today the way we forgive ourselves is the way we allow God to forgive us. If I never hear myself say, "I forgive you Joe," how am I going to believe God when He says, I forgive you and I have placed your sins behind you. Isn't there a reason then, that Jean-Jaques Rousseau can say, "Man was born free, yet everywhere I look, I see him in chains."

Many people do not forgive themselves for some action in the present or actions in the past: stealing, lying, cheating, lack of respect for parents and authority figures, premarital sex, adultery, or abortion. You can also carry a burden of guilt not because of an action, but because of your non-action at a crucial juncture. If you had had the vision or courage to say or do something, then someone else might have been spared great pain. (Anam Cara) Once you began to see what your failure to act actually allowed, you feel guilt and shame. Somewhere we need to be able to say, "I forgive you." We need to bring our guilt and shame to the Sacrament of Reconciliation and then accept the words that we are forgiven. This forgiveness, God's forgiveness, will depend so much on how we forgive ourselves. Lack of forgiveness will deprive us of enjoying God's gift of forgiveness. Forgiveness is God's gift to us. We must impart the gift of reconciliation to ourselves. Reconciliation is a process, not an event. It is a lifelong journey because of the experience of being human.

To help us on the journey into reconciliation, it is very helpful to write, **not type**, a letter of understanding and forgiveness to yourself for the actions of the past which we are finding hard to accept and forgive now. With understanding comes forgiveness. To help us with understanding we need to go back and place ourselves in those events and circumstances which are causing us difficulty right now. We are told in Philosophy that the object of the senses is good. We will never do anything that at the moment of doing does not appear to be good. Five seconds, five minutes, five days, five years later, we see that was not the best decision, but it was the best decision at the time we performed the actions.

We did our best, just not the best in those situations. Again, with understanding comes forgiveness. Hindsight is always 20/20. We can judge ourselves harshly in our 30's and our 40's about actions we did in our teens and 20's. We need compassion, not condemnation. In *Anam*

Cara, by John Donohoe on page 117, we read, "Every person has certain qualities or presences in their heart that are awkward, disturbing, and negative. One of your sacred duties is to exercise kindness toward them. In a sense, you are called to be a loving parent to your delinquent qualities." After you write your letter of forgiveness, burn it, not tear it up, burn it.

So let us use the season of Lent to deal with the guilt of the past and impart in ourselves the gift of forgiveness, reconciliation and freedom. Let us bestow on ourselves the gift of compassion, so we can enjoy God's gift of compassion and understanding. Paul tells us in Corinthians, "Love is patient, Love is kind, Love takes no offense and is not resentful." Let us use this season of Lent, to put those four aspects of Love into our daily life, into our daily living. We will then walk beyond guilt and fear, into freedom and a transformed sense of who we are in God's love. Our goal is always to be able to love ourselves as God loves us. When we do not forgive ourselves, in other words, allow God's forgiveness to penetrate into what can be a hardened heart. It is wonderful to keep in front of us the following words of Henri J. M. Nouwen:

> "God's mercy is greater than our sins. There is an awareness of sin that does not lead to God but to self-preoccupation. Our temptation is to be so impressed by our sins and failings and so overwhelmed by our lack of generosity that we get stuck in a paralyzing guilt. It is the guilt that says: 'I am too sinful to deserve God's mercy.' It is the guilt that leads to introspection instead of directing our eyes to God. It is the guilt that has become an idol and therefore a form of pride. Lent is the time to break down this idol and to direct our attention to our loving Lord. The question is: 'Are we like Judas, who was so overcome by his sin that he could not believe in God's mercy any longer and hanged himself, or are we like Peter who returned to his Lord with repentance and cried bitterly for his sins?' The season of Lent, during which winter and spring struggle with each other for dominance, helps us in a special way to cry out for God's mercy."

When we have a God of mercy we have a loving God. In fact we have a God that is prodigal in His love for us. He is reckless, extravagant with the merciful love He offers to you and me in each and every moment of our journey to Him and with Him. Conversely, if we do not have a God of mercy, or worse still when we see ourselves as not needing a God of mercy, there is a kind of hell in which we have placed ourselves and then blamed others and God for it.

Let us remove the stumbling block of guilt so we can see deeper into the cave of our soul where the presence of God is always there to forgive, to reconcile and impart to us the gift of freedom, the gift of new life which will enable us to live more deeply what is ours because of our baptism. Please love yourself enough to give yourself this gift of forgiveness. Only you can allow yourself to enjoy the gift of forgiveness already offered to you by your God. Psalm 103, "As far as the East is from the West, so far have I put your sins behind you." In the Old Testament we are told in Isaiah, "You have thrown my sins over your shoulder." The following was written by Merton to Henri Nouwen, which many people have embraced, resulting in a new freedom and a new happiness. "At the center of our being is a point of nothingness which is untouched by sin and by illusion, a point of pure faith, a point or mark which belongs entirely to God...this little point...is the pure glory of God in us...it is like pure diamond, blazing with the invisible light of Heaven. It is in everybody."

Our God and Father is a God who is prodigal in His love for us. Let us give ourselves the freedom to leave behind the prison of guilt, so we can walk more freely knowing His eyes are watching, His ears are listening and we truly have a Friend by our side. A Friend who will never leave us or abandon us.

Free Will or Won't

In *The Battlefield of The Soul*, (below) we read, "My Free Will." Our free will, we are reminded, is a gift freely given to us by God. He will never interfere with this free will. And God will not take our free will away. At times, we wish we didn't have it. We would then have no chance of making mistakes – taking the wrong road.

The Battlefield of the Soul

MY FREE WILL:
Given out of Love

<u>Toxic Trinity</u>						<u>God's Dream -</u> <u>The Aisling of God</u>		
	........The saboteur					........Father		
The Father of Lies	........The prosecutor				The Holy Trinity	........Son		
	........Sarx (Paul's Flesh)					........Holy Spirit		

I CHOOSE
EVERY MOMENT

Control	Power	Hatred	Earn	Guilt		Faith	Light	Unconditioned	Wisdom	Time
Comparison	Property	Violence	Deserve	Fear		Hope	Life	Unlimited	Empowerment	Attention
Competition	Prestige	Death	Qualify	Shame		Love	Love	Unrestricted	Transformation	Tenderness

Death Dealer-Victim-Wounded Wounder   Wounded Healer-Survivor-Life Giver

Oh God, help me to believe the truth about myself
No matter how BEAUTIFUL it is.

We could say to God, "You do everything. I'll just be along for the ride. I expect it's going to be a good one because it's all up to You." To do this is to surrender our free will. To surrender our free will, under any circumstances, is a sin. Our free will is that which makes us human. When we don't act as healthy human beings, we revert to acting like animals. Our God-given ability to think and act makes us rational animals. We are not puppets. So each and every moment of each and every day, we have to make choices. Those choices are made either consciously or subconsciously.

We read in the Scriptures that we're presented with life and death, good and evil. Whichever we choose will be given to us. So, in every moment, we are going to be life-givers or death-dealers. Will we choose a life lived as the *beloved*? When we choose that life, we live a life that is permeated with the light, life, and love of God. When we deny ourselves that gift, we are choosing to live a life of guilt, fear, and shame. One choice is a life lived in the freedom our gracious God has chosen for us. To choose to live a life locked in the prison of guilt, fear, and shame is the life of a *victim*, not that of the beloved.

We sometimes hear it said of a judge in our courts, "He takes into account all sides of an issue." Not all judges are like that. Some work out of a personal agenda with injustice as a result. But our God is a just God. Again in the Scriptures, our God "understands man and woman's every deed." Our God understands us better than we understand ourselves. He loves us more than we ever can imagine or hope for. He looks at us through the eyes of infinite mercy and compassion.

Jesus had a real problem with those who were rigid and inflexible. He called the Scribes and Pharisees a bunch of hypocrites. Jesus wasn't being a "nice guy." He was being honest, much to the Pharisees' chagrin. The Scribes and Pharisees were caught up in "religiosity", and Jesus was telling them how hard and difficult it is for the self-righteous to get into The Kingdom. The Kingdom is for the poor, the broken, the sinner – a concept the Scribes and Pharisees were either unwilling or incapable of accepting.

Now here is the nasty part: the Scribes and Pharisees are alive and well, and have taken up residence within us. When we are lured into the lie that we must earn, deserve, or qualify for our God's love, we have joined their group. When we compare ourselves to others so as to relish the feeling of being better than they, guess who is in charge?

Jesus did not come to this Earth and assume a perfect humanity. His humanity is the same humanity we share; no different. He continues to use that same imperfect humanity today, through us, to carry on His mission and His ministry. Our spiritual journey is a conscious effort to acknowledge that we are beaten and bruised, just like He is. For some reason, our God has chosen this way to reveal His presence to us and to the world. This is the "wisdom of God" that makes no sense to this world, and it made no sense to the Scribes and Pharisees. It is our calling to struggle day-to-day while His mystery of grace brings about The Kingdom, using our mistakes and blunders as the main instruments of its creation. It is not for us to analyze how it happens. It's up to us to allow grace to flow. Enjoy the mystery as it unfolds. It's up to us to surrender to the process and develop an attitude of celebration as we journey on our unique hikes though this mysterious life-giving creation. Every moment of God's Creative Love molds us and fashions us into a living image of His son, Jesus Christ. The great miracle of grace in our weaknesses and brokenness is what allows us to see the passionate merciful love of our Father. So again, enjoy and above all else, celebrate the hike.

As Fr. van Kaam, C.S.Sp. explains,

'The Lord wants to incarnate Himself in the world through persons involved there as fully human beings. My daily environment should not be looked upon as the Divine, but a possibility of entrance into the Divine. Every new enterprise, reading or encounter may reveal to me another aspect of God's presence. I should never identify one task, place, or assignment with God Himself or see it as the only road to God. In that case, I might suffer from religious fetishism, which means that I isolate one specific person or place and tell myself that this is the only road to God for me. If I do so, I may be in danger of closing myself off from the rest of reality and remain fixated on one or more parts of my total situation. In such estrangement from reality, both my daily and spiritual life may become fiction."

Chapter 5:
Up the Mountain

On a Wednesday morning, as is my custom, I turned to the sports page of the paper. An article that caught my eye featured a reporter joining John Lott, the Arizona Cardinals Strength and Conditioning Coach, and his team's encounter with Camelback Mountain. There was something about the article that resonated with me. I finished breakfast and went about my errands.

As the day went on, the connection between what Lott wants to achieve for the Cardinals and the deeper meaning of our life's hikes became clear.

Lott's vision for that journey up and down Camelback was to instill not only strength and endurance into his players, but to teach them perseverance. All of those qualities are necessary for a football team. But these qualities are essential in the fourth quarter of a game when a tackle must be executed or the winning drive is demanded of players. I'm sure there were moments on that mountain when the desire of team members cried out "QUIT," but a higher power – John Lott – would not allow that to happen.

As on the mountain, so too on the field, players realize the pain they endure is for a higher purpose, and they suck it up. In moments of great struggle with human limitations, we somehow gather strength from some special place in order to achieve a goal. In Lott's players' case, something clicked for them which spread to others. There is that voice that says all those moments of painful struggle in June are meant to prepare me for the games ahead. In November, when the best efforts of authentic human beings are demanded, these athletes know they have what it takes to succeed. They know what it means to be in the "zone." In the language of the spiritual life, we call that serenity.

Most of us don't have the opportunity to meet the challenge of Camelback every day. However, we often are presented with challenges far greater than what is encountered on a trek up a mountain. We may face loss of health and energy, or we may be asked to journey with a loved one who meets that challenge. Whether it's the burdens of unemployment, the lack of health insurance, the uncertainly of a new relationship, the pain of loss and betrayal – any of these may push many human beings into a "victim role" rather than that of a survivor.

Living life as a victim is pure hell. My definition of hell is "a place where there is no love." This is the place where there seems to be no hope; there is no light at the end of the tunnel. But there is, however, the still and quiet voice that emerges from the depths to whisper: "This is not my lot in life. I have been called from all of eternity to live a life of freedom, not fear. I will be a survivor." In this struggle, the truth is spoken. The lie is named. Light has appeared out of the darkness. And in this struggle, we experience on a deep level the journey of Jesus as told by St. Luke. Carroll Stuhlmueller has written: "Luke's 'journey narrative' is…a symbolic way, a literary device, to combine several journeys; Jesus' and our *own*, through the mystery of death and resurrection. The events in Jesus' ministry become the way by which we follow as disciples. Luke, therefore, wants to jar us into the realization that this is *our* journey, so that the passion and resurrection of Jesus becomes a living, transforming reality within us."

Acceptance

I was able to pick up Fr. Rolheiser's great book, *The Holy Longing*, at a bargain price in a thrift shop. (On a side note; Thrift shops are my favorite haunt. I have been able to buy some great books and wonderful music at unbelievably low prices.) There are two fantastic chapters in the book. One chapter is on the Spirituality of The Paschal Mystery, and the other is on the Spirituality of Sexuality. Both of these chapters are a daily read.

In this book Fr. Rolheiser quotes Henri Nouwen:

"Our life is a short time in expectation – a time in which sadness and joy kiss each other at every moment. There is a quality of sadness that pervades all moments of our life. It seems there is no such thing as clear-cut pure joy, but even in the happiest moments of our existence, we sense a tinge of sadness. In every satisfaction, there is an awareness of limitations. In every success, there is fear of jealousy. Behind every smile, there is a tear. In every embrace, there is loneliness. In every friendship, there is distance. And, in all forms of light, there is the knowledge of surrounding darkness. But this intimate experience in which every bit of life is touched with a bit of death can point us beyond the limits of our existence. It can do so by making us look forward in expectation to the day when our hearts will be filled with perfect joy, a joy no one shall take away from us."

Then Fr. Rolheiser writes his commentary:

"What Nouwen affirms here, in simple language, is what Christian Theology means when it tells us we are living in the interim eschatological age. We are living in that time between Christ's Resurrection (the initial triumph of God's promise to give us fulfillment) and the final consummation of that promise – the end of time (when all tears will be wiped away).

During that time, and it is an interim time, we will always live in tension, waiting for the final consummation of history and our lives. Our happiness depends not on overcoming this, which we cannot do in any case, but in making peace with it. But that peace is not made by a stoic acceptance that we cannot have it all in this life. It is made by living our incompleteness in the face of a future promise.

To live in the interim eschatological age is to be like a couple waiting to be married who, for a good reason (for example; the death of a parent), have chosen to postpone their marriage for a period of time. There is a certain frustration in that delay, but that frustration is offset by the clear knowledge that this is only a temporary delay, soon to be overcome. Our essential "inconsummation" in this life must be understood in this way. The frustration is real, but it is, as Nouwen so well puts it, "something we will one day overcome, albeit that day will not meet us in this life."

Our spiritual journey, then, is living in that reality every day. Fr. Rolheiser hits it right on the head when he points out that we are dealing with real frustration, and that frustration is *now*. We can't overcome this frustration by fighting it. That battle would be futile. We can't win. Or we can't overcome it by making attempts to fix it. But somehow, it is in accepting the frustration that we are able to arrive at a place of peace. I'm talking about acceptance of whom we are and who God is. God is God, and we are not. We have a great, deep desire, given to us by our God, to be totally one with Him once again. But that journey begins with our search for who we are. And in that process, we find union with Him, who is our Source, and Destiny.

The Psalmist provides us with those wonderful lines, "out of the depths I cry to you O Lord, Lord, hear my cry." When we allow ourselves to taste the essential helplessness, hopelessness, and powerlessness of whom we are as human beings, our Savior, God, will then come to us with these consoling words, "My Beloved, here I am. I am always standing beside you. I will not – I cannot – desert or abandon you. You are to me as beloved as your brother, Jesus. The love I have for the both of you is the same." Can we believe that? It is not this reality that we have difficulty with? It is only through a deepening of faith that will bring us to that place. It is ours to have. Ask and we shall receive; seek and we shall find; knock and it will be opened to us. Always keep in mind, "My ways, are not your ways. My time is not the way you figure time. I will come at a time and in the places you least expect. It has been this way, and as it was, so it shall ever be."

I believe, Lord. Help my unbelief/disbelief.

Feeding the Spirit

I am adding here a further reflection on the sacramentality of Spiritual reading and why it is so essential for a healthy spirituality. To form a healthy spirituality, investigating what others have discovered is extremely helpful. This journey is the work of the Holy Spirit, and so can be trusted. None of us are comfortable facing the honest truth that is part and parcel of this journey. There is consolation in the adage, "we are as sick as our secrets." The more we grow in honesty – and honesty is cumulative – the freer we are to enjoy that which our God has dreamed for us. Our lives are not boring.

Spiritual reading does this for us. It is a blessing and a curse. It is a sacrament (with a small "s") in the sense that each and every person, place, event, and action that brings us in touch with the deeper realities of life and ultimately with Reality Itself, is the reality we call God.

We are in constant need of being reminded of whom we really are. We need to have that constant reinforcement of our innate dignity. Why? Because Satan, the father of all lies, wants us to believe in the lie. The lie is that we are not who we really are called to be; we have to earn, deserve, and qualify for the unconditional love of God. But that love comes to us in so many ways and through so many channels.

Fr. Rolheiser has written of The Incarnation:

"When Jesus walked around Palestine, people were healed and forgiven, not to mention given eternal life, by touching him and being touched by Him and simply by relating to Him. If we are the ongoing incarnation, and we are, then this is true also for us (and not just in the sense of it happening through the institutional churches, important as that is). The mystery of the incarnation is extensive. It is not just the institutional churches that carry on, carry forth, and carry the mystery of God in human flesh. ALL LOVE THAT IS IN GRACE IS THE WORD MADE FLESH. To touch it is to be touched by Christ; to touch with it is to touch with Christ because it is the ongoing incarnation. From Augustine through Pius XII, we are told that this is wild doctrine; something beyond our limited imaginations and measured hopes. Nobody dares hope for us as much as God has already given in the incarnation."

"What are we given there? It gives us the power, literally, to block death and hell. If we love someone, that person cannot go to hell because Christ is loving him or her. If we forgive someone, that person is forgiven because Christ is forgiving him or her. If children of ours, or anyone else we love, no longer goes to church, our love for them and their love for us binds them solidly to the Body of Christ. They continue to touch the hem of Christ's garment as surely as did the woman in the gospel who suffered with a hemorrhage. The end result, unless they reject their bond to us, will be like hers; namely, healing. It is Christ who is doing this. We, as St. Paul so clearly assures us, 'are the body of Christ.' He recognizes how difficult it is for us ordinary people to believe, accept, and act upon."

So he concludes with these words:

"Part of the difficulty in believing in the incarnation is precisely the fact that it is too good to be true: God is not hidden or hard to contact; forgiveness, grace, and salvation are not the prerogative of the lucky and the few; we do not have to live our lives perfectly to be saved. Human flesh and this world are not obstacles but part of the vehicle to heaven; we can help each other on the journey; love, indeed human love, is stronger than death; and to love someone is indeed to say, 'You at least will never die!' "

This spiritual reading does take us deeper, and so it is indeed sacramental. This will lead us to pray for simple faith, to believe in the very simple words of Scripture.

The question is then, who are you?

God Walks His Talk

There is a prayer each day in the paper. One day, it read:

"Lord, each day let us look for and find good news to give to others we meet, so we may help spread Your love and light to those around us. Amen."

It was later in the day when I began to read the Scriptures for the weekend's liturgy. The following is from The Book of Wisdom.

"You have mercy on all, because You can do all things; and You overlook the sins of men that they may repent. For You love all things that are and loathe nothing that You have made; for what You hated You would not have fashioned. And how could a thing remain unless You will it; or be preserved, had it not been called forth by You? But You spare all things because they are Yours, O Lord and lover of souls, for Your imperishable Spirit is in all things! You rebuke offenders little by little, warn them and remind them of the sins they are committing, that they abandon their wickedness and believe in You, O Lord."

Now that is real good news. It is such good news that it can stop us in our tracks. God loves all that He has made. Yes, there is nothing that God has made that His love does not maintain in existence. If it exists, it is loved all the time. God's love is permanent and does not waver. Whereas, the love we experience and express is all over the place. It runs hot and cold. Lukewarm, however, is the killer. Jesus has a warning for the lukewarm.

Revelation 3:16 *"So because you are lukewarm, neither hot nor cold, I will spit you out of my mouth."*

Our God hates nothing that He has made. That's an eye opener for those individuals who use God as a weapon to impart their own guilt and shame onto those with whom they have difficulty. How often God is used as a weapon for evil when all there exists in God is infinite understanding, mercy, compassion, and abundant love. How we see and treat others reveals a great deal about our own selves. We infrequently see a person as that person truly is; we generally see them as we see ourselves. Nobody can see us as we really are. Even we ourselves cannot do that. Only God sees us as we are.

Our God always sees us through the lens of His love. What a terrible act of abuse it is to use the All Loving God as a weapon to suit our own agenda. When I have difficulty with someone, it is not actually with that individual; it is, sadly, about me, and I do not want to deal with me. Eventually, we will have to come home to whom we really are and discover that all humankind dwells within each one of us.

In keeping with that, Jung says, "Everything that irritates us about others can lead us to an understanding of ourselves." All that irritates me allows me to fall into the love we are told about in the Wisdom reading.

We all have heard about those who walk the talk, and those who talk the walk. It could be said that God in the Scriptures is talking the walk. In the Gospels, we see that Jesus has come to walk the talk, and in doing so, is calling on us, His followers, to do the same thing. Our God hates no one, but maintains us all in His love.

Jesus became the incarnation of that love. His message of acceptance was so radical that it got Him killed. His outreach was so extraordinary, His own family wanted to intervene. In the Gospel, Jesus scandalizes the self-righteous with His acceptance of the invitation to eat a meal with a sinner. The word "sinner" was the same as prostitute. Those whom Jesus had reached out to were the tax collectors, the sinners, and the prostitutes. Jesus pointed out that the tax collectors and prostitutes heard and accepted His word. On the other hand, those who stood in judgment of all *three* did not.

Our God always keeps us and reaches out to us in His love. The more we find the tax collector and sinner deep within ourselves, the deeper we will fall into the love revealed to us by *Love Incarnate*, Jesus

Christ. We will then be able to go beyond snap judgments of others and reach out in understanding and compassion. In this human encounter, the mission and the ministry of Love Incarnate will continue. Let us take the risk of expressing the desire to be able not just to talk the walk, but also to walk the talk. We become what we desire. What a ride; what a journey that will be.

"May the changing moods of the human heart and the limits which our failings impose on hope never blind us to You, source of every good." Mass Prayer.

It is only through the lens of the tax collector and sinner that we will eventually arrive at that place where we will find ourselves dining with Our Lord and Savior, Jesus Christ. Does God have a sense of humor or what? In the last place we expect to find Him, there He is, looking at us and asking the question, "What took you so long?"

❄ Chapter 6: ❄
Switchbacks

*In 2009, I hiked the Mallard Creek trail. It was my first hike to Mallard Lake.
To be honest, I had some reservations about this choice.   A ranger informed
me that the lake trail was "a little more challenging" (translation: a steeper
trail). She was quick to add that the scenery was so much better. When I
heard the word "steeper," I immediately countered with the question, "Are
there any switchbacks?" She replied with a reassuring smile,
"Yes, there are." What a relief.*

On difficult hikes, I look forward to the switchbacks. They provide time and space to regroup a little and gather the energy and strength needed to meet the challenge of the next stage of the climb. As it is on hikes, so it is with the *hike* we call "The Spiritual Journey."

On hikes we take, we can't plan switchbacks; nature has control over them. However, on the hike of our everyday lives, we are in control (and only we are) of where those switchback moments exist for us. However, we call those who don't take this healthy step of self-control "victims." They put everyone else before themselves. They have no healthy self-love. They are often used, abused and set aside by others. Their energies are used up quickly. Their talents and resources are exhausted. There is nothing left in their lives except shame, anger, and resentments. Victims respond to what happens to them by being human doers. But those who take the healthy step of self-control are called "survivors." Survivors have a healthy sense of personal boundaries. They know when it is in their best interest to say "yes" and when to say "no." They obey the command, "Be still and know that I am God." Survivors demand respect. They are not people-pleasers. They demand to be treated as human beings, and they believe that God created us to live our lives as free *human beings.*

Well, let's get back to the hike. What a hike it was. Otherwise, I wouldn't be writing about it. As I made my way up the trail, I was struck with the peace, calmness, and serenity of my surroundings. I don't know why this was so. Was it because I was in a good place, or was it the trail itself and all that it had to offer? I believe it was both.

The trail was somewhat challenging, but soft and gentle underfoot. I bounced off the sod as I moved along. It was great – so wonder-full that I thought this trail should be named "The Serenity Trail to Mallard Lake."

I journeyed along, lost in thought, enjoying the feeling of being immersed in Yellowstone. I gradually made my way up the trail. Not only were there switchbacks; there were also little hills. I was really enjoying myself while keeping a close eye out for Mr. or Mrs. Bear. Earlier in the week, I came within about 20 yards of a bear! I wasn't able to determine whether it was a Mrs., a Mr., a Miss or a Master Bear, but the bear shot off very fast! Take it from me, bears are agile. I'm so thankful that it decided to run away from me and not at me. I'm told they can hit speeds of 35 to 40 mph. Later in the week, I saw a huge grizzly. He was about a quarter of a mile away. I tucked him away in the safety of my camera where he wasn't a threat.

Now there I was, lost in thought among the trees. However, I had no view of the sky, and that's not good. Suddenly, I heard the sound of thunder in the distance, so I thought it wasn't anything to worry about. So I went back to being lost in the joy and pleasure of the hike. Then there was another peal of thunder. This one got my attention, because this time, there was lightning before the thunder rolled. I looked up and saw that the sky had darkened in the east, but there was blue sky to the west. So I headed for the west keeping the thought of the blue sky uppermost in my mind, and not paying too much attention to the darkness. Not even a few raindrops got my attention. Not a smart move. I failed to read all the signs of an impending storm.

I hadn't made the right decision, as usual, and there was a price to be paid. Of course, this wasn't the first time in my life that this happened. And I have every reason to believe it won't be the last. As long as I am a limited human being, it will happen again and again until the day I die. It is our friend, death, who will free us to live the fullness of life. In the meantime, we are to struggle on a daily basis with what it means to be "a spiritual being having a human experience."

Well, the few raindrops became a downpour. So here I was at somewhere between 7,500 and 8,000 feet. There was wind, rain, thunder and lightning. To make matters worse, the rain turned to hail, and it was freezing cold. I had not been in this kind of weather since I left Ireland. In Ireland, Mother Nature would never play a trick like this. Here I am in the summertime, and winter enters to darken an otherwise joyful experience. But it is never a lasting darkness. When light appears again, as it always does, what will be the truths that become a part of the new reality? This new reality is "life as I live it today."

Divine Encounter

How would I get down the mountain safely? What was the lesson to be learned apart from the obvious?

As my hands began to go numb, I marveled at how quickly the

serene ascent transformed into stark discomfort. Sometime later, I came across a fitting description of my adventure: "Beauty serves to prepare the soul for an encounter with God." That trail, which was such a sacrament, revealing the presence and the mystery of God in the beauty of His creation, had changed. The trail is still a sacrament. However, it demands more in-depth thought – lots of thought and reflection. It is in the storms of life we need the x-ray eyes of faith to see the deeper meaning behind the obvious reality of pain, stress, and discomfort. The rain and hail sure made that trail different and more difficult. I had great confidence on the way up. But as the rain began to gather and flow downhill, I had to go slow and carefully choose my steps. The rocks that I avoided on the way up the hill became a source of security on the way down. Those same rocks stopped me from slipping and sliding. The same can be said of the rock we call faith. What was once in our youth a source of discomfort for us – prayer, the Mass, the Sacraments, moments of quiet reflection – now become a source of peace and serenity. What were once seen as obstacles are now seen as stepping stones. "Storms in our Life," I believe, reveal their own sacramental value to us as well.

Life Happens

A person of my age and temperament must be cautious. That peaceful and serene trail became a great challenge. As I began the descent, I skipped about to avoid the puddles. (Now that was a sight to see – my version of a jig.) After a short time, I realized that was a useless attempt since my boots were getting soaked. I couldn't help thinking to those days in my childhood when I thought how great it felt to jump into puddles, much to the horror of my mother She wasn't appreciating my great joy; all she could see was the washing and ironing that was awaiting her as a result of my great adventure.

Well, there I was, happy as could be, splashing my way downhill in the rain, wind, hail, flashing lightning, and rolling thunder. There was a tremendous feeling of renewed innocence and inner freedom that came with the buffeting. I was warm in my body, and my energy was strong. It was good to be alive, and I wanted to keep that feeling. However, when the lightning got really close, I wanted to get to a shelter and wait the storm out. It was getting late. I had no idea how long that storm would last. The sky looked as if (as we say in Ireland) "It was settling in for the evening." So I continued on down that wet, sloppy trail which in some places turned into a stream.

Some parts of my body were numb and freezing cold while other parts enjoyed the long forgotten pleasures of playing in the rain. I was anxiously looking for familiar signs along the way down that would tell me how much farther I had to go. I breathed a great sigh of relief when I saw the trailhead sign. I knew I was close to the parking lot and soon would feel the warmth of my car. I reached the car and turned on the heat. Then I took out a change of clothes, had something to eat and headed for home. It rained the whole way home.

I've had many opportunities to reflect on that hike. How true to the spiritual life that experience was. How often do we find ourselves going along in a state of bliss? From our perspective, life is going well. All our ducks are in line; our plans are working out; our expectations are, for the most part, being met. Most of the people in our lives are walking in step with us. That's was me on the first leg of the hike. Then life happens. We become aware, or in some cases are forced into awareness, that our spiritual being is completely immersed in the totality of the human experience. The storm that hit me on my physical journey will hit us all on our spiritual trek as well. When I'm lost in the storm, I realize there is no place to go; that Jesus has not abandoned me. He is there waiting for me to show up. Christ also became weary on His journey when He was buffeted by the storms. He was disappointed. As the Scriptures say, "He was like unto us in all things except sin," and He died out of love for us sinners.

As human beings, we can so easily go from calm and serene to angry and spiteful in a split second. We can go from accepting to resentful in no time flat. Being Irish, I sometimes think it's my nature to act first and then think. I have to learn to be a "responder" rather than a "reactor." I'm still learning that one. I have to learn to slow down and read the signs of the time in which I find myself.

On my hike, the changes around me were gradual, and I overlooked them. I was so caught up in the good feelings of a great hike that the reality of my situation was ignored. My emotional needs for joy and happiness were met while at the same time I put myself in physical danger. When my rational side finally took over, I made the healthy decision to take the trail home. I have to learn to balance my emotional and my rational responses to issues. How often the signs of danger and trouble are there, but we choose to ignore them rather than to confront them. How often are we so unaware of disasters that will happen if we continue in our dysfunction. To make matters worse, we blame God for what happens to us and where we are in the moment. God has nothing to do with the trouble and danger in which we find ourselves. It wasn't God who led me into that danger through what was an apparent good. It was my responsibility to take all factors into account and to make a rational decision. On the next hike, I was pretty far out on the trail when I looked up and saw the dark clouds. The trail looked great in front of me, and it was very tempting to go "just a little farther." However, this time I turned back. I barely made it to the car when the heavens opened. Enough said.

Failing and Falling

As human beings, we fall again and again. Falling and failing are inevitable qualities of our human condition. In many and various ways, we encounter the pain that accompanies failure. So it's essential for us is to have a place where we feel warm, safe, and secure – a sanctuary, as it were, where we can express our sorrow and, when necessary, shed our tears. We all are in deep need of that place where we receive a welcoming embrace; a caring arm around our shoulder; a reassuring, strong hand. Such a place is essential for our psychological and spiritual health. We each must have that place, that person, that sanctuary, where we are embraced in our tears and fears without questioning, restricting, or judging. When we find ourselves in that hurting place, we want to receive a warm embrace without conditions; a place where we can cry without being judged. We want to feel that it's okay to be sad, angry, disappointed, teed off (to put it politely) without anyone saying, "You shouldn't feel that way." Instead, we want to hear, "You are not alone. I'm here for you and you're safe." And above all, "you are loved – you are loved as you are right now." We want to know we are not strangers or aliens, but rather we are loved as we are and where we are. In other words, we want to be the *Beloved*, His beloved. We are asked to remember that it's not about how we see or feel about God; rather, it's about how *God* sees and feels about us. We seem always to sell God short. As St. John says, "It is not about us loving God; it is about God loving us." It is *not* about our giving love; it is about our *receiving* love. The beloved does not earn, deserve, or qualify for the love of the Loving One. All that the beloved can do is surrender to the love offered by the *Loving One*. This interchange is a lifelong process.

"Every time you listen with great attentiveness to the voice that calls you the Beloved, you will discover within yourself a desire to hear that voice longer and more deeply. It is like discovering a well in the desert. Once you have touched wet ground, you want to dig deeper. I have been doing a lot of digging lately, and I know that I am just beginning to see a little stream bubbling up through the dry sand. I have to keep digging because that little stream comes from a huge reservoir beneath the desert of my life."
—HENRI NOUWEN

Chapter 7:
Thrown for a Loop: End & Begin Again

"Isle of Hopes, Isle of Tears,
Isle of Freedom, Isle of Fear,
But it's not the isle I have left behind."

These words are taken from a haunting Irish immigrant song. They describe the land of promise – America. For this immigrant, these words also describe the America I have come to experience and know. I arrived in 1963 shortly before President Kennedy was killed. Those were dark days of uncertainty. They were the precursor of other days of fear and struggle. Who among us will ever be able to forget the disastrous day of September 11, 2001?

Yet, into that darkness came a little light and a glimmer of hope. Christina Taylor Green was born on that fateful day when the world as we knew it ceased to exist. A new world was encountered and lived in. Christina's birth was God's way of saying "despite what may happen, I am still involved in My Creation. I haven't lost confidence in humankind. See, I am sending a new source of My Presence. I am sending this new creation as a reminder that there will always be goodness entering into creation. My creation will continue." On that day in 2001, when more than 3,000 people died, a new life began. Less than 10 years later, when an attempt was made on Congresswoman Gabrielle Giffords' life, Christina was one of those killed on that day. And so a life so full of energy, enthusiasm, hope and dreams also came to a sudden end. This ending began a new way of living for Christina.

Christina returned to the infinite love that created her nine years earlier. We have to endure dealing with her absence and the questions surrounding her death. Death, because it is a sacrament, will trigger questions about what is true and what is real. Death will always make us question the reality of our own existence and the values that shape our life. On that day of tragedy when so many people died, Christina's life began. What a life she shared with her family, friends, school, parish, and community. She had set her sights on a life of service and leadership. We, as a church, a state, a nation, were drawn into her life and left with a sense of awe and wonder. St. Irenaeus said many centuries ago: "The glory of God is the human person fully alive."

We were gifted with God's presence in and through the life of Christina. That is a reality hidden and revealed in each and every life. Christina made God look really *Good*. We will have to rely on that same God of goodness to become our living Savior. There is a beautiful prayer that's part of the liturgy: "Almighty and ever-present Father; your watchful care reaches from end to end and orders all things in such power that even the tensions and tragedy of sin cannot frustrate your loving plans." We need to make that prayer our daily prayer. We must ask for a real deepening of our faith in what the prayer says. It's a prayer of confidence in the fact that God's power is greater than all the forces of hatred, prejudice, bigotry, and cynicism. The Spirit that was the source of Christina's vitality is the same Spirit that was imparted to us the day we were baptized. Christina was the model of what could happen. We have the opportunity to continue the good she began. As we do so, we will continue the mission and ministry of Jesus who became the Christ. Then we will understand that death is not an end; it's the beginning of a new and different way of living.

Blessings

When there is an ending in your life, there is always a new beginning. A loss brings a new set of lenses. I have always believed that death leads us to question the authenticity of our existence. It makes us question what has lasting value. Loss makes us reflect on the value of what couldn't see but only felt. Loss and feelings are a tough mix. We don't always allow ourselves the gift of grieving a loss. And when we don't grieve a loss, we miss out on so many blessings because of the time we spend focusing on our new and transformed existence. We're in need of lenses which enable us to become more and more aware of all our blessings when a life supposedly ends. Our faith assures us that life has no beginning and no end.

We have come from the Eternal Life Community of Father, Son, and Holy Spirit. We share that eternal life and love, always and everywhere. We need people in our lives who are constant reminders of who we are as the beloved.

The following is from Nouwen's *Life of the Beloved*.

"Let me first tell you what I mean by the word "blessing." Latin to bless is "benedicere." The word "benediction" that is used in many churches means literally: speaking (dictio) well (bene) or saying good things of someone. That speaks to me. I need to hear good things said of me, and I know many of you have the same need. Nowadays, we often say: 'We have to affirm each other.' Without affirmation, it is hard to live well. To give someone a blessing is the most significant affirmation we can offer. It is more than a word of praise or appreciation; it is more than pointing out someone's talents or good deeds; it is more than putting someone in the light. To give a blessing is to say "yes" to a person's "Belovedness." And more than that, to give a blessing creates the reality of which it speaks. There is a lot of mutual admiration in this world, as there is a lot of mutual condemnation. A blessing goes beyond the distinction between admiration and condemnation, between virtues or vices, between good deeds or evil deeds. A blessing touches the original goodness of the other and calls forth his or her Belovedness."

The blessings that we give to each other are expressions of the blessings that rest on us from all eternity. It is the deepest affirmation of our true selves. It is not enough to be chosen. We also need an ongoing blessing that allows us to hear in an ever-new way that we belong to a loving God who will never leave us alone, but will remind us always that we are guided by love every step of our lives.

The movement of God's Spirit is very gentle, very soft – and hidden. It does not seek attention. But that movement is also very persistent, strong, and deep. It changes our hearts radically.

When was the last time you reflected on those who have blessed you? When was the last time you blessed your children? S/he is the same baby you got up to feed in the middle of the night. Were you not blessed by those moments of mystery when life's nourishment flowed from you to the newest manifestation on the Divine Presence? What has happened in the meantime? No matter what has happened in the family dynamic, that child is still, and will ever be, the Beloved of our common Source of Being. It again goes back to the lenses we are looking through. Have you ever asked for your child's blessing?

I wonder what asking for his/her blessing would do to the relationship. It would be a moment of Mystery being present. Each person has the God-given power to bless. In the midst of laughter, peace, and quiet, why not add to these good feelings. Why not make prayers of shared blessing an *essential* part of the lives we share with those whom God has chosen to journey with us. We are beloved, and they share the same belovedness. Why not celebrate on a regular basis that which we have most in common. Let's celebrate what we have in common rather than wasting time wishing and wanting for what is not there. God is not present in the wishing and wanting. God is only present in the reality of the here and now.

As I look back on my life, I am caught up in the gratitude for all those people, places, and events which have been a source of blessing for me. I encourage everyone to think about what blessings you have received throughout your life. As we come to accept the blessings we've received, there comes the overwhelming realization of "how blessed I am." Why not share that blessedness with those people our God places in our lives, and let the process begin all over again? What great faith and trust our God has in us. On the other hand, what else would we expect from *The Loving One*?

Hope

As with most adventures in life, hikes have a beginning and an end; an ascent and a descent, unless, of course, we are on a loop. In the spiritual life, ascending has to do with the realm of the spirit, while descending has to do with the work of the soul. My spirit and soul got a great workout on the Mallard Lake hike. Actually, I could say there were two hikes in one. The ascending was in the peace and security of clear skies and bright sunshine. This lifted my spirit into the realm of freedom; freedom from care, concern, fear, and worry. It was so natural to say "Thank You." An attitude of gratitude was so apparent. The descending was much the opposite. It was a journey into insecurity, fear, and concern. This was, and is, the journey of the soul. Soul work is not really appealing. That's why the spiritual journey is not attractive to many people, because inevitably, there's soul work, and soul work is hard work. On my hike, I was given a deeper insight into both. Isn't this the way we spend all of our daily living? We don't have to go on a hike to have this experience. We experience both sides almost every day.

There are some days – even some moments of our day when we are in sunshine. We safely say, "I've got this life thing wired." When we are in that much desired place, Fr. Rohr calls it "inflation." But we never stop there. We then go to the opposite pole or extreme. Here, we meet the challenge of being lost, lonely, and so isolated that we ask the questions, "How did I get into this mess?" and "Is it ever going to stop or go away?" This pole, at which so much of our lives are spent, is called "alienation."

When we are at that the alienation pole in our daily journey, we are really frazzled. We do not know which way is up. We often face the limits of our endurance. Here, we border on hopelessness and helplessness – but we are in the best place possible. Yes! Contrary to popular belief, we are in the best place possible – *Spiritually*. This is where our ego doesn't want to go.

The ego will do everything in its power to avoid this situation. The ego has the power of the devil on its side. And what do we have on our side as we slowly come to admit our human limitations? We are guaranteed *The Power of God* that overcomes all evil. However, we have to face what the ego hates – the great challenge we call surrender.

That's why soul work is so repulsive to the ego, and also to us who want to look good and powerful. Here we face what Fr. Rolheiser calls the "challenge of our insufficiency." Here we are challenged to face our own inner incompleteness. For the ego, a root canal is more acceptable.

When I returned to my cabin from a tortuous hike, I had a great big bowl of soup. Did that taste good! Later, I had a relaxing hot bath. That night before I went to bed, I enjoyed a big mug of chamomile tea. As I lay there feeling very safe, cozy, and warm, I had to ask myself, "Can this get any better?" To make things even more sublime, I was in that state where I knew I was falling asleep. I suffer from insomnia, so this was the cherry on the sundae. I fell asleep listening to the wind and the rain – my very favorite sounds. It was great to experience that feeling of contentment. The big question that was begging to be asked was, would it last? Of course not, I'm sad to say. Within a short period, I was back facing my essential loneliness, insecurity, incompleteness, and discontent. I was again back in the daily struggle of what it means to be a spiritual being having a human experience. Thank the Good Lord, this is not our lasting home; we are only here on a visit. So in the meantime, we have our daily struggle. There's no escape.

Fr. Karl Rahner explains: "In the torment of the insufficiency of everything attainable, we come to understand that here, in this life, all symphonies remain unfinished."

Fr. Rolheiser extends the concept in his commentary:

"What does it mean to be tormented by insufficiency of everything attainable?" How are we tortured by what we cannot have? We all experience this daily. In fact, for all but a few privileged, peaceful times, this torment is like an undertow to everything we experience. Beauty makes us restless when it should bring us peace; the love we experience with our spouse does not fulfill our longings; the relationships we have within our families seem too petty and too domestic to be fulfilling; our job is hopelessly inadequate to the dreams we have for ourselves; the place we live in seems boring and lifeless in comparison to other places; and we are too restless to sit peacefully at our own tables, sleep peacefully in our own beds, and be at ease within our own skins. We are tormented by the insufficiency of everything attainable when our lives are too small for us and we live in them in such a way that we are always waiting, waiting for something or somebody to come along and change things so that our lives, as we imagine them, might begin. To be tormented with restlessness is to be human."

I have found great consolation and courage in those words.

Become a Butterfly

Acceptance is tough, hard, and difficult, but it is the only real road to an ever-deepening spiritual life. Acceptance of whom we really are is first and foremost a process. A process we all, or at least for me, seem to make every effort to avoid.

Is this the reason there is so little use made of the Sacrament of Reconciliation?

Reconciling the good and evil which exists within each one of us is a very painful process. But the one gift that can make this process worthwhile, however painful, is gut honesty. We grow slowly in the acceptance of that deep honesty of whom we really are. This process is made somewhat easier when we have a person in our lives who bestows unconditional, unlimited, and unrestricted love on us, especially in times when we have abandoned whom we really are out of toxic shame. That toxic shame wants to send a message contrary to our deepest reality. The message of toxic shame is "we are not good enough, we are not smart enough, we are not beautiful enough, and blah, blah, blah". All of that is a *Lie*, and the source of the lie is "the father of all lies" – Satan. When we listen to the voice of toxic shame, we are giving ear to the Devil rather than to the voice of the Spirit of Truth. Because God is Truth, this Voice of God tells us from deep within that we are loved as we are without conditions, restrictions, or reservations.

This battle rages on and on and on within us. It's our constant struggle. We have to make a choice every moment. "Am I the beloved of God with all that it means?" or "Will I be duped into the lie that I am not, and never will be good enough?"

These questions lie ever before you and me. "Will I work on being spiritually healthy and live a life of freedom as the beloved daughter/son of the Loving One?" or "Will I live out my life in the unmitigated hell of being spiritually sick?" The popular word for that today is co-dependent. This means I will choose to live my God-given life not with the real God as my guide, but replacing that God with the dis-eased view of a limited human being.

A healthy relationship is always pointing to *The Love* relationship between us and God. It is to embrace freedom, peace, love, joy, and happiness as by-products of this mysterious reality. Yes! Happiness is a by-product. A healthy relationship is the cocoon from which emerges the wonder-full, beautiful butterfly which is who we are in God's love. The butterfly is destined to fly free; that's our destiny as well.

Does this healthy relationship with God – this freedom to fly, automatically happen every time for each of us? Sad to say, it doesn't. But don't fear. We are given what it takes to fly free. We are given the ability to make healthy choices. There are times in our lives when we will have to let go of controlling people so we can walk in the freedom of whom we really are. We'll have to establish boundaries with individuals who have no concept of boundaries. We'll have to say, "I love you, but I cannot have you in my life," and stick with that decision despite all the feedback from friends and family.

I recommend Cloud & Townsend's book, *Boundaries*. As a jumpstart, go to a bookstore and read the chapter beginning on page 103. That will give you permission to live your new life of freedom which is God's wish for you. Then check out the chapter starting on page 83 and discover a powerful message.

I am reminded of a cartoon that graced my office door at St. Andrew for many years. A man speaking to a woman, says: "I liked you better before you learned to love yourself."

Mother…Motherhood…is a Sacrament

There is an awe-full, mysterious, sacred presence in our lives. A presence, I am sad to say, that seems to be acknowledged, reverenced, and celebrated just one day out of 365. As we live out the other days, is not this mysterious reality taken for granted? Has the place of our encounter with the Sacred become so familiar that we have lost our reverence, and respect for this God-given gift?

That is the danger of the familiar, it leads us into that death-dealing place of apathy. We are always in the need to be awakened to the sacred, to the mysterious that is part and parcel of our everyday journey–the journey that is ours as spiritual beings immersed in the human condition. Within the depths of our mothers, an encounter takes place, between the creative love of Creator God, and the human effort of human beings, acting freely. This hidden, sacred, mysterious encounter has led to the present day understanding of the sacramentality of sexuality. We have surely come a long way in our growing understanding of human sexuality and the sacramental aspect of this gift.

Now we go a step further and are asked to reflect on the sacramentality of mothers and motherhood. I'm referring to sacrament with a small "s." A small "s" sacrament I would like to suggest is: " Each and every person, place, event, action, which brings us into contact with the deeper realities of life, ultimately with Reality itself, that Reality we call God." The sacramental reality of mothers and motherhood must be visited again and again. Like all that is mysterious, this journey leads us to a deeper understanding of that which can never be explained, only reverenced. We find there is layer upon layer to the mystery that is "mothers" and "motherhood." Just stop and reflect on all that has been written, and is being written. It is never-ending, so we must be open to ever new, life-enhancing, life-enriching revelations. Speaking of revelation, the scriptures have some wonder-full passages offered for our encouragement.

Our Father/Mother God, in Isaiah 49:15 "Can a mother forget her infant, be without tenderness for the child of her womb? Even should she forget, I will never forget you." So we are forever present in the minds of God, and to a lesser extent to our mothers. There are times when we will be absent from the conscious thought of our mothers, after all, they do have their own lives. In the mind of God we are always present to Him, as we journey with Him, and to Him. Our Father/Mother God is our origin and our destiny. "Before I formed you in the womb I knew you" Psalm 110:3, "from the womb before the day star, I have begotten you." Our place of origin then is the womb of God, Who is infinite love. We leave that place of comfort and security and journey into the uncertainty that is this life. God has not abandoned us. He has prepared for us a presence who will remind us of whom it is we came from, and the love from which we originated.

The loving Gaze of mothers is the loving gaze of God enfleshed. This is a loving presence we can feel, hear, and above all be touched by. This soothes the pain of the seeming loss of our First Love. Our mother is to mirror the first love, and who we continue to be in that love. The best of plans do not always work out, not even God's "plan A". We are in His "plan B". There is a dark side to mothers and motherhood. The ideal in so many cases is never actualized, and this results in human beings existing in a "living hell." Because of abuse, some women's essential inner wholeness has been broken, and in some cases destroyed. There are so many books written about "Daughters without Mothers," and the recovery necessary to return to wholeness. Thank God for the courage of those authors who tell their stories and offer hope to those who have to face this reality in their lives.

There are many sons without mothers as well. There is so much healing to go through to journey back to the place where you were the beloved. We must not allow transient evil to sabotage our essential goodness and lovableness. That recovery, like all recovery, is not easy. Toxic shame will fight us each and every step of the way. Toxic shame which wants to communicate that we are not okay, somehow not "good enough," has to be faced. We are all more than we do, or have or achieve. We therefore need the unconditioned love, undeserved, unlimited "first love" to become a reality. In this way, while we are still pilgrims, having no lasting home, we are somehow secure in the knowledge that our God is always nourishing, ever creative, ever comforting, and always ever mercy-full. Why? Because we have experienced all within the lives who reveal the Mystery within mothers and motherhood. Mothers, you are the living sacrament of our living God. Be healthy so we can have a healthy understanding of, and a healthy relationship with The Source, The Origin. We will then find ourselves living the aisling, the dream of our Mother/Father God.

❧ Epilogue: ❧
Moving On

All of us have left the place where we were one with God and we were one with one another, in the love of God. We have left that place that is our original and permanent home to enter into our second and transitory home of our human experience. Like all exiles, we carry with us a memory of the first home; our first Holy Family.

Being in exile is a struggle. I can truthfully tell you that from my own experience of living a life in exile for 48 years. The memories of home and loved ones are always with you. From time to time, your heart aches for the familiar. The familiar home voices, accents, streets, neighborhoods, and above all, the countryside. The exile is an exile forever, until a home, a sanctuary of the spirit, is created. That creation, like all creation, is an ongoing process. The process demands we connect again and again with the Aisling of God, the Dream of God, for us as individuals, as family, and as the family of humankind. We must allow the light, life, and love of God to guide our path as we make this journey, all while a sanctuary is being created. This creation is the work of grace – God's love in action. This is a journey – a process we create one moment at a time. It's a journey we take one step at a time. It's our mysterious, sacred hike.

A few times on a hike out-of-state, I have come across fellow Irish exiles on the trail. The sound of accents from our greetings led to each of us questioning, "Where are you from?" The response resulted in a lengthy conversation because it takes an Irish person at least five minutes just to say "Hello" and "How is it going?" There is joy and laughter in the conversation. The conversation is always tinged with sadness because we each know, as good as this is, it is going to end. There has to be "a moving on." Because of the encounter, we move on a little lighter in our steps; our spirits brightened by the exchange with a fellow exile.

"The savage loves his native shore, though rude the soil and chill the air, well then may Erin's sons adore. Their isle, which nature formed so fair."
— JAMES ORR

Exiles need fellow exiles. To my way of thinking, our Father must have looked down on us, His exiled children, and what He saw moved Him to compassion. He saw us at times lost, dispirited, scared, lonely, disconnected, and battered by feelings of alienation and abandonment. So He sent His son into exile with us. A son who came emptied of the trappings of divinity so that He could be immersed and enabled to embrace all that it means to be human. Jesus, God in exile, embraced our humanity. He embraced it to the point where He, too, knew what it was to be lonely, abandoned, betrayed, scared, and hungering for human companionship. He not only drank from the cup of our humanity, He drained it to the last drop, to the bitter end.

So we are not threatened, God comes to us as a vulnerable baby. It is as if to say to us, "I am not here to scare you, to threaten you, to trigger feelings of guilt, fear and shame. I am here to remind you of the love with which you have been loved from the very beginning – the love from which you came and the love to which you shall return. Of all my creations, there is no newborn more vulnerable than the human child. Here I am – I am with you. That is why I am called Emmanuel. I am here to live with you – to suffer with you and to die for you."

Nouwen imagines what Christ, our Guide on life's journey, says to you and to me:

"I have called you by name. From the very beginning, you are mine and I am yours. You are my Beloved; in you my favor rests. I have molded you in the depths of the earth and knitted you together in your mother's womb. I have carved you in the palms of my hands and hidden you in the shadow of my embrace. I look at you with infinite tenderness, and I care for you with a care more intimate than that of a mother for her child. I have counted every hair of your head and guided your every step. Wherever you go, I go with you; and wherever you rest, I keep watch. I give you food, I will satisfy all your hunger and give you drink that quenches all of your thirst. I will not hide my face from you. You know me as your own, as I know you as my own. You belong to me. I am your father, your mother, your brother, your sister, your lover, and your spouse...yes, even your child. Wherever you are, I will be. Nothing will ever separate us; we are one."

A dreamer's journey continues....

About The Author

Joseph I. Hennessy was born in Ireland in 1939 to parents, Patrick and Mary Ellen (O'Sullivan). He attended six separate schools between ages 4 and 17, leaving friends and neighbors behind each time, which had a deep influence on his approach to parish ministry. His father was a policeman (Garda) in the Counties of Cork and Tipperary. As a cousin of famed resistance leader Michael Collins, Hennessy was raised on stories of struggle for freedom and independence.

Mary Ellen was diagnosed with tuberculosis in 1938 and spent 48 weeks in the hospital. Her hope of having the child for which she had ardently prayed appeared to be crushed. However, after a pilgrimage to Lourdes, she returned home cured of the disease that had killed her mother. Joseph was born the following year, suffering no ill effects from the crude medical treatments of the time. His upbringing was a blend of Catholicism and Celtic tradition. His parents each supported different political parties and practiced distinctly different approaches to their faith. Mary Ellen was deeply religious and Patrick deeply spiritual. His mother grounded a young Joseph in the strict practice of Catholicism while his father gave him "the great gift of wonder." Wonder indeed.

Ordained in June 1963 at St. Patrick's College in Carlow, Ireland, Hennessy's faith was burnished in the upheaval that surrounded Pope John XXIII and Vatican II. His goal: survival in a new environment that was edging away from rigidity toward the challenge of inclusion; from a focus on strict obedience to a kinder, gentler welcoming of community. The change meant drama, trauma, and finally, transformation. Hennessy likens the seismic shift to an imaginary rollercoaster at Disneyland – full of twists and turns over a 50-year vocation, but ultimately worth the ride.

His journey has taken him to the American Southwest and several parishes throughout Arizona, which reflected the diversity and the socio-economic climate of the U.S. His pastoral career included the founding of St. Andrew the Apostle Parish in 1986 and being honored in Patrick Brennan's 2002 book, *Parishes that Excel in America,* as shepherding one of the nation's two most successful Catholic Christian communities. It was also highlighted in the National Conference of Catholic Bishops' "Best Practices in Catholic Formation." Hennessy's journey, focusing on nurturing the "little church of the home," centers on embracing people "where they are" and sharing their faith through caring, sharing, welcoming, and daring. In 2000, he was instrumental in establishing the Interparish Catholic Elementary School of St. John Bosco in Phoenix.

Hennessy retired in 2007, but maintains a full schedule of ministry, writing and traveling. He is the founder of The Aisling Educational Foundation whose mission is to enable youth "who do the most with the least" to pursue higher education. Proceeds from the sale of his books fund scholarships to aid Catholic students in Arizona and in Haiti.